Mindfulness
Tools for Gay
MEN
In Therapy

A Clinician's Guide for Mind-Body Wellness

Rick Miller, LICSW

"Rick Miller's *Mindfulness Tools for Gay Men* is not just a book on mindfulness. It is also a highly intelligent compassionate guide to understanding the psychotherapy needs of gay men. Tackling all the most challenging topics with which gay men struggle, from self-esteem to sex to HIV status, relationships, and spirituality, he uses mindfulness to make the journey affirming and compassionate. Using guided meditations, he invites his clients to 'befriend' their fears and shame, heal the wounded places inside, and access their authentic selves. This excellent book not only teaches skills but heals the heart."

-Janina Fisher, PhD,
Author and internationally renouned trauma expert

"Helping gay clients come to self-acceptance and self-knowledge can be a powerful pathway to healing and positive change. Rick Miller has combined mindfulness and therapy for gay clients in this practical and comprehensive workbook. It has scripts and all you need to be more effective and confident in working with gay clients. A unique offering by a skilled and kind-hearted writer and clinician."

-Bill O'Hanlon, MS,
Author of *Pathways to Spirituality and Do One Thing Different*

"Rick Miller's *Mindfulness Tools for Gay Men in Therapy* is a must-have guide for clinicians wanting to grow as they bring a deeper level of understanding, awareness, and sensitivity into their work with gay men. Mindfulness challenges us to embrace an open hearted, truth-seeking, and, compassionate approach to life—and this book gives you the mindfulness tools necessary to take your client on a journey to authenticity and transformational wellness. I highly recommend this for clinicians using mindfulness."

- Donald Altman, MA, LPC,
Author of *The Mindfulness Toolbox, 101 Mindful Ways to Build Resilience*, and *Clearing Emotional Clutter*

"This workbook offers fellow therapists guidance, information, and answers, just as I know Rick Miller offers support and compassion to his clients. How refreshing for therapists to have a book that provides the vocabulary and the permission to connect with gay clients in a direct, empathic, and more-informed way."

- Lynn Lyons, LICSW,
Author of *Anxious Kids, Anxious Parents and Using Hypnosis with Children: Creating and Delivering Effective Interventions*

"This is the only book written that incorporates mindfulness specifically for gay men. Rick Miller provides exercises that therapists can use to remind clients that their pain doesn't need to define who they are. With the help of this workbook, instead of relying on external sources for reducing shame, gay male clients can learn how to access authenticity stemming from a position of internal mastery, perhaps for the very first time."

- Joe Kort, PhD, LMSW,
Author of *10 Things Gay Men Can Do To Improve Their Lives*

"Rick Miller does an excellent job of educating therapists about gender and the subculture that gay men live in. The book delves into the complexities of being gay, defining day-to-day struggles but also those that have been hidden due to growing up gay. I love the fact that the book provides scripts and a "how to" approach to healing and mental health."

- Anne Fausto-Sterling, PhD,
Author of *Myths of Gender: Biological Theories about Women and Men*

Published by
PESI Publishing & Media
PESI, Inc
3839 White Ave
Eau Claire, WI 54703

Cover: Amy Rubenzer
Editing: Blair Davis
Layout: Bookmasters & Amy Rubenzer

ISBN: 9781683730224

Printed in the United States of America.

 PESI Publishing & Media
www.pesipublishing.com

BIOGRAPHY

Rick Miller, LICSW is a clinical social worker in private practice in Boston and on Cape Cod, Massachusetts. He has served on the national and international faculties for the International Society of Hypnosis, the Milton Erickson Foundation of South Africa, the Brief Therapy Conference, the Society for Clinical and Experimental Hypnosis, the American Society of Clinical Hypnosis, the American Group Psychotherapy Association, and Harvard Medical School.

As part of his international presentation calendar, Mr. Miller was an invited lecturer at the University of Johannesburg Department of Psychology, Johannesburg, South Africa. He also developed a curriculum for hypnotherapy with gay men, used by both the Milton Erickson Institute of Mexico City and the National Autonomous University of Mexico.

Mr. Miller's popular blog, *Unwrapped: Mind-Body Wisdom and the Modern Gay Man*, is featured on *Psychology Today.com*, and his work has appeared in *Psychotherapy Networker* as well as *Somatic Psychotherapy Today*. His first book, *Unwrapped: Integrative Therapy with Gay Men*, was published in 2014, and he was a contributing author to the book *For Couples: Ten Commandments for Every Aspect of Your Relationship Journey* (2011). www.rickmiller.biz

ACKNOWLEDGMENTS

Oren Sherman, for his support, pride, and encouragement—and for his tolerance of my endless hours at my desk.

Suzi Tucker, whose generosity and knowledge complete my sentences.

Jeffrey K. Zeig, for his continued belief and trust in me and for sharing a lifetime of amazing networks.

Thomas Egan, for the complex wise reminder about the meaning of home.

Karsyn Morse, who welcomed me to PESI.

My New York City master class family, without whom I would not be here now.

Clients, for what they teach me and how they appreciate the power of shared mindful moments.

Truro, Massachusetts, in wintertime—the perfect backdrop for inspiring thoughts and creativity.

Daisy Mae, for waiting until 4 pm to begin her "c'mon Rick" pacing, because a 3:30 break is non-negotiable.

My MacBook Air: You invoke struggle but also happiness.

CONTENTS

1 Therapy, Mindfulness, and Your Gay Male Client

When a gay man comes for psychotherapy, his identified issue is almost always going to be nested in the fact that growing up gay is fraught with deep personal suffering. In a world that is largely unprepared to guide a gay boy, self-inhibition is a navigational tool that he is likely to develop very early. Thus, your gay male client has been editing himself since childhood—though you may not see it and he may not realize it. There are few people with whom he can be his true self, few environments in which he can feel fully at peace. A lifetime of negative messages from society at large and within the family cannot be undone by a gay-affirmative television show or the striking down of an antiquated marriage law. Gay men need to gain new experiences of safety in inhabiting the present fully; this is true of just about every gay man who walks into your therapy office.

The time is ripe for a book dedicated specifically to mindfulness and other experiential work with gay men. Until now, therapists have had to borrow from generic mind-body approaches when working with their gay male clients. This book will allow therapists to offer insights and experiential opportunities that are tailored to gay men's specific challenges and questions.

As therapists, it is our responsibility to be educated about the people we see. Our waiting rooms do not discriminate, and it is very unlikely that any therapist will go through an entire career without opening the door to a gay male client. In my role as an educator, it is compelling when therapists are willing to admit that they don't know everything they should about what it is to be gay or how to work with gay clients. It takes courage to admit this, especially in the new climate in which sexuality is front and center in the national conversation.

It is my plan to fill in many of the gaps in understanding regarding the gay man's journey and to provide a host of practical interventions to support his well-being. Needless to say, most therapy has moved away from a perspective of gay = pathology. Now it is time to cultivate the ways in which health and happiness can be seeded across all dimensions of life for our gay male clients. I will help you help your gay clients turn this next corner.

LET'S START WITH SHAME

For gay men, shame is a birthright. It is the pervasive consequence of internalizing the negative reflections that come from family and society. These reflections have so many masks—fear, hatred, embarrassment, ignorance, judgment, mocking, belittling—and they lurk in every corner of the client's life. You can bet that the avoidance of shame is the driving force for him.

Your client may not even be aware of it, compartmentalizing so successfully that he is hidden even from himself.

Finding a way to align with clients with these experiences is part of the creative task for the therapist. Ultimately, it is the client's ability to acknowledge his pain and then to experience new comfort inside of his own body that will begin to convince him that well-being—truly being well—is within reach.

Even though the foliage on a tree may appear vibrant, it is the root system that provides nurturance. Long before he is even verbal, a gay male censors the truth to make sure he is loved and accepted. This is a reflex, automatic and unconscious, for survival. Therapists must always have this in mind as gay clients describe current challenges. The roots cannot be seen; they are underground. One component of psychotherapy with gay men is to appreciate the causes of damage to the root system. Then, the gift is to offer tangible ways to make repairs. It is never too late to restore the flow.

THE BODY MEANS BETRAYAL

Something to remember is that the body has meant betrayal for gay men as they were growing up and beyond. The body carries the memory of being different from other boys. Later, this body may not fit the media ideal promoted for men in general or the specific ideal gay male stereotype. And, certainly, the body is a traitor when it brings illness and sometimes death through its interactions.

Even after being out for years, many gay men continue to hide parts of themselves. They split off certain parts in an attempt to fit in. Gay men are unique in being a minority not only in the world but also in their own families. I call the need to conceal aspects of who one is "hiding in." Gay men often take shelter deep inside a fortified place, separate from others.

But at what price? The fortified heart eventually becomes impenetrable, and most gay men continue to carry this way of being into adulthood. The trauma of being gay in an uncomprehending world is something a person doesn't simply "get over"; decades later, hiding stills seems to be the way to stay safe. This kind of safety has a cost, which is manifested in various ways.

SAFE OUTSIDE BEGINS WITH SAFE INSIDE

Over the decades, I have developed a way to accompany my gay male clients as they move out of hiding. It begins with identifying resources my clients already have, with an acknowledgment of their resilience and faith in themselves. I point out that I know that these things exist in my gay male clients, not because I am especially intuitive but because my clients are sitting across from me having survived and garnered enough resources to bring them to the present moment. Focusing gently in an informal way on the internal foundation my clients have already established, I take an opportunity to celebrate this accomplishment with them.

Mindfulness is an especially helpful perspective and practice for gay men, but it is scary at first. For a gay man, self-trust has in the past led him astray into discomfort and perhaps danger. From a very young age, he knew he was different, and he likely learned very quickly that his "difference" was unacceptable to family, to friends, to community, to God. Thus, dissociating from his instincts and from his difference became the compass and the map. After a lifetime of evidence to the contrary, he must be convinced that connecting to himself in the present is the more secure, healthier approach.

Mindfulness is key to well-being for gay men. Impulsiveness, bad habits, and self-destructiveness are all rooted in dissociation. The promise of mindfulness is in creating the circumstances from which thoughtful decisions, good practices, and constructive choices can emerge. Once your client experiences some of the strategies in this workbook, he will understand the essential place of mindfulness from the inside out. More than good advice, mindfulness invites him to experience himself as the wise and caring mentor on which he ultimately will be able to rely.

Simply begin with breath and a positive memory. A few quick questions about the positives in his life will help the client take the first steps toward being mindful: Perhaps he has a new job, takes care of a rescue dog, has finished a painting, has graduated from college, has learned to ski, visits his ailing father regularly, volunteers at the library, ran in a marathon . . . anything about which he feels good.

Introducing Mindfulness to Your Client

DIRECTIONS: Emphasize the following points in promoting the efficacy of mindfulness. You can ask your client to rate which of these apply to him, give examples of how other clients have incorporated mindfulness and how it helped them, or share your observations of how mindfulness will help him with his issues of concern.

Mindfulness helps people to:

- Cope with or reduce symptoms related to anxiety and depression.

- Manage physical discomfort, symptoms related to illness, or the manifestations of stress in the body.

- Calm the mind, as staying attuned to the present moment has a self-regulating effect.

- Open themselves to the totality of experience rather than numbing themselves to day-to-day experiences in an effort to cope.

- Make decisions by going inward and allowing the collective wisdom of body and mind to inform them about potential actions that are needed.

- *Feel* instead of using defenses as an avoidance technique.

- Connect with others in a meaningful, available manner.

Comfort and Breath

DIRECTIONS: The following exercise provides an introduction to mindfulness benefits. You can gently instruct your client to find a comfortable space and close his eyes. If closing his eyes is too threatening, simply have him focus on an object and soften his gaze. Practice this short mindfulness exercise as a way of introducing your client to mindfulness so he can have an experiential awareness of how it works.

"Find a comfortable space by allowing your body to get into a relaxing position. You can choose to sit or lie down, perhaps imagining yourself outdoors in nature where the scents or sounds may help you center yourself.

With your eyes closed, you begin to appreciate how your awareness shifts ... further and further away from the moments or pressures of your day, closer and closer to your own abilities to observe and be present to what is happening inside of your body in this moment. Excellent.

As I count from one to five, simply allow each breath to be a little bit deeper than the last one, focusing on the inhale and the exhale, and while you do this, enjoy the ways in which you can go deeper and deeper inside: 1 ... 2 ... 3 ... 4 ... 5. ***That is right—the outside pressures of your day recede further and further away."***

[Pause a few moments.]

"And now as I count backwards from 5 to 1, you can slowly orient yourself back into my office, feeling rested and refreshed, appreciating that even in a quick series of moments, you were able to experience a transformation that came to you rather easily.

When I finish counting back to 1, you may slowly and gently open your eyes and bring yourself back. 5 ... 4 ... 3 ... 2 ... 1."

ANOTHER VARIATION

For this variation of the basic mindfulness exercise, help the client focus on a moment in which he felt strong and capable.

"As you think about the time that you _____, you realize that it signifies a moment in which you overcame your hesitance and experienced being truly capable; breathe in that feeling. Breathe it in to reach every part of your body, every cell. We can use an easy count of four: 1 . . . 2 . . . 3 . . . 4.

And now, you may hold this feeling inside, filled, and I will be your witness. Let it fill your chest and your abdomen for another easy count of four: 1 . . . 2 . . . 3 . . . 4.

Now, as you release your breath slowly, let any tension or anxiety flow out with it. Let's give it time, a count of eight: 1 . . . 2 . . . 3 . . . 4 . . . 5 . . . 6 . . . 7 . . . 8. The lightness will remain as you let go of any tension. We can repeat these cleansing breaths several times. We have time. And you can take this small exercise with you, reclaim it any time: It will be right here at your service, any time, within you."

This little meditation marks a beginning as you and your client imagine how to reset his compass to navigate his current life rather than the terrain of the past. It is helpful for you as his therapist to discern for yourself the primary ways in which the client has dealt with life in the past and what is reasonable now given his background, age, physical condition, and other factors.

POSITIVE ATTRIBUTIONS

DIRECTIONS:

The following list reflects some of the ways in which your gay client has experienced or navigated life until now, including paralysis, anxiety, rigidity, loneliness, alienation, and invisibility. This exercise will help you clarify the type of defenses your client has honed over his lifetime and, more importantly, how to guide him toward updating the ways in in which he navigates his life.

Taking into account the vocabulary of your client, create a list of positive experiences or attributes that you will help him achieve to allow him to move beyond the parameters of his earlier defenses.

1.

2.

3.

What types of interventions will you use to help him reach these goals? Why do you expect these particular approaches to be beneficial to him?

1.

2.

3.

How will you and he know that he has shifted his original position or gained more appropriate tools?

1.

2.

3.

ABOUT THIS BOOK

There has never been an interactive book that focuses on mindfulness techniques created specifically for gay men. Why is it important? Because mindfulness is the practice of being in the moment, but if the moment doesn't feel like a safe place to be, the practice cannot have power. This book is designed to bring together therapy and experiential practice with crucial insight so that therapy has a chance to penetrate the complicated internal and external matrices in which gay men live their lives.

The scripts come directly out of my clinical practice with gay men. They are inspired by the work I do and the experience I have both as a professional and as a gay man. I offer the scripts as a guide. Setting aside some time for a script will deepen the session, amplifying the felt experience of important moments.

You can build your confidence in using the scripts by starting with shorter ones, and as you develop your ease, you may use the longer ones provided in each chapter or create your own. You will see that your clients begin to look forward to the feeling of calm that is engendered by the scripts and appreciate that this feeling can be expanded outside the therapy room as you teach them how to use the tools and strategies of mindfulness on their own. You will intuitively learn how and when to use the scripts as you fall into good rhythm with your clients' receptivity.

> ## EACH CHAPTER IN THIS BOOK
> ### COVERS THREE REALMS:
>
> 1. **PSYCHOSOCIAL ISSUES, QUESTIONS** for you to ask yourself as clinicians, and **OPTIMAL INTERVENTIONS**
>
> 2. **WORKSHEETS** and **HANDOUTS** for clinicians and/or clients
>
> 3. **MINDFULNESS SCRIPTS** to use with clients

The mindfulness practices I teach along with my whole-life therapy approach create life-changing shifts for my gay clients. The shifts are visible immediately as I work with a script and see a sense of profound relief washing over a client. I am always awed by the impact, and the client is usually surprised by his experience of sudden release. Perhaps never before has he felt the peace and relaxation that can occur as the mind and body are aligned. The need for vigilance softens in these moments. **The client's face transforms as self-connection and self-awareness take root. Years of suffering and protection fall away. Something new appears: possibility.**

> **For your convenience, you may download a PDF version of the worksheets in this book from our dedicated website: go.pesi.com/Miller**

2 | The Gay Man's Journey: From "Being Better" to "Being Well"

BEGINNING TO MAP THE NEW TERRITORY

For gay men, the pain never goes away completely.

Even for a client who came out a long time ago and has a successful career and a good connection with friends and family, something may be not quite right just beneath the surface. This may manifest as depression or perhaps stress or anxiety. With your help, as your client pays close attention to difficult feelings, he can usually pinpoint where they are in his body. The harder part for him to understand is why the feelings exist at all. If the feelings are kind of manageable, why even bother doing something about them? Why not just keep busy and distracted? After all, this is how men often cope. Still, the client knows, as you do, that there is a way to address difficult feelings, to release them, so that they don't gnaw away at his insides as he distracts himself with other things.

As I teach and practice mindfulness with my gay clients, real comfort begins to land in them. The fear of connection that has been a guiding light for so many years begins to ease. The armor that has rigidly been carried for protection can soften as the client's core emerges. Years of tension start to leave his face as the muscles relax and self-trust begins to shine.

There are certainly good books on treating gay men, and there are thousands of titles on wellness in general, but until now, there hasn't been a book on how these topics are folded into each other. Why is that? I suspect it has to do with the relatively short history of the acceptance of gay men in our society. Contemporary literature highlights the importance of no longer pathologizing gay experience. However, an emphasis on wellness (not just the absence of pathology) is a few rungs up that ladder—something that we as therapists treating gay men need to consider. It is time. The unique therapeutic model presented here focuses on fostering wellness for gay men in daily living, helping them to flourish despite their painful histories, and creating new possibilities for fulfillment and emotional freedom.

Gay men may have succeeded professionally, achieving stability and abundance in the public sphere, but the heartbreaking memories of growing up gay are always lurking like shadows. As therapists, we have a chance to help gay men step out from those shadows. Through sensory awareness and a practice of identifying and appreciating wellness in the moment rather than dwelling on the past, gay men can look forward with a clear lens and renewed energy.

9

INTERNALIZED HOMOPHOBIA

The term *internalized homophobia* refers to holding a negative view of homosexuality in one's own psyche stemming from societal beliefs. Gay children who are fearful or homophobic may disown their own gay impulses and identities rather than acting on them. Such hiding bleeds into adulthood.

Every gay male possesses some internal form of homophobia. He may not think about it or notice it, but it exists and stems from shame. One simply cannot grow up in a world that overwhelmingly reflects back negative images of being gay—or no images at all—and emerge completely grounded in a confident, positive sense of self.

Internalized homophobia sets parameters that are sometimes deeply subconscious. The client's choices may be powerfully or more subtly driven by it:

- He does not allow himself to live out and openly and instead subscribe to a traditional lifestyle that is not aligned with his whole self.

- He is overly concerned about mannerisms that he deems too effeminate or theatrical.

- He worries about his wardrobe choices seeming "too gay" (i.e., stylish and contemporary).

- He does not share details of his personal life with others, such as with whom he spends time on weekends, or he doesn't use pronouns when referring to significant others.

- He criticizes men who are viewed as being gay or flamboyant.

- He makes intentional (or unintentional) choices to fit in.

- He changes voice tone when he is with heterosexual men.

- He rejects other gay men who bring out his own self-loathing.

Not recognizing these types of fear creates an overall feeling of discontent, discomfort, and confusion.

A Mindful Moment

The key to honest self-reflection is the ability to relax the body and mind enough to access feelings and thoughts with ease and without judgment. Pausing to let the client rest into this moment with you before doing the self-assessment exercise will provide the ground he needs to feel safe and confident.

IS YOUR GAY MALE CLIENT
A VICTIM OF HIS OWN SELF-HATRED?

Ask your client to complete the following assessment worksheet (with you or on his own), in which he will check off the best response to each question to help you and him to assess the degree to which he experiences internalized homophobia. This informal assessment will open up powerful conversations about inherent biases that affect his sense of wellbeing in hidden ways. This can be an effective first step in utilizing mind-body work with a client, as you begin to discern with him a shift from discomfort to comfort.

DIRECTIONS FOR THERAPIST:

- Have your client find a comfortable position in his chair where his body is supported and air can flow.
- He may close his eyes or keep them open.
- Guide him through some deep, easy breathing.
- Ask him to allow his mind to clear. You can let him know that he can go back to his problems later, but in this moment, nothing requires his attention.
- Gently assure him that in this state he will easily be able to be self-reflective.
- Remind him that solutions for his well-being are born of mindful moments.
- Ask him to open his eyes (if they were closed) and to reorient.
- Have him complete the following questions.

Client Self-Consciousness

DIRECTIONS: Circle the best response to the following.

1. Do you feel self-conscious in certain settings where you assume you are the only gay man?

   Never   Sometimes   Usually   Always

2. Do you find yourself holding back from self-expression and making choices in an effort to fit into mainstream society?

   Never   Sometimes   Usually   Always

3. Do you leave out details of your social life when speaking to family members or coworkers?

   Never   Sometimes   Usually   Always

4. Do you ever worry about what to wear or modify your wardrobe selection in order to fit in better?

   Never   Sometimes   Usually   Always

5. Do you find yourself changing your tone of voice or curbing gestures in certain contexts?

   Never   Sometimes   Usually   Always

6. Do you criticize men you find to be stereotypically effeminate?

   Never   Sometimes   Usually   Always

7. Do you make fun of these men (with others) as a means to gain approval?

   Never   Sometimes   Usually   Always

THE EXPERIENTIAL REALM
AS TRANSFORMATIONAL

Gay males achieve inner alignment from mind-body work based on a developing awareness that the body can be a friend. For many clients, this understanding is completely new, and they will have to get used to it. Giving your client opportunities, perhaps for the first time, to visit internal spaces through quiet moments, deep breathing, and the mindfulness exercises provided here is key to galvanizing his internal resources. Most people can imagine the benefits of mindfulness, but gay men may be completely shocked by these benefits, as they have so often rejected the body as a traitor, except for sexual expression. Your gay male client will respond positively to what feels magical and extraordinary, as he gains new access to the body as a container for calm and confidence.

Mindfulness is an experience—something felt, not just heard or talked about. Mindfulness enlists all dimensions into an integrated present. Experiential work can awaken the force of internal power, which then shines out into the world.

THE PURSUIT OF HAPPINESS

Learning to look inside for abundance rather than outside for validation can be the key to happiness. This practice may allow your gay male client to:

- Generate his own solutions to issues
- Gain a new feeling of control over his life
- Move into ease and away from rigidity or anxiety

Perhaps he is doing experiential work for the first time in his life. You will be emphasizing his internal resources. This may be disconcerting for a client who isn't aware of how much strength he already possesses. You will help him discover, expand, and eventually trust these internal resources.

THERAPIST AS TOUR GUIDE:
THE JOURNEY FROM UNDOING TO REDOING

Bear in mind that the quality of the relationship between therapist and client is a primary factor in the success of psychotherapy. You are inviting your client to go inside, directly or perhaps indirectly suggesting that there is abundance within him of which he may not be fully cognizant. This powerful experience that takes place inside the client's body, involving all of his senses, is what I call *undoing and redoing*. With your help, he experiences a rejuvenation of his ability to experience delight, and two things happen simultaneously: He is undoing the old, internalized way of being. He is in therapy to work on his presenting issue and get solutions through the process of experiential work, which in itself is powerful. Even more importantly, he is redoing. On a deeper level, he is waking up an internal aliveness through the experiential work that can incorporate wholly fresh possibilities. Offering a chance to create space inside for the real self to emerge, rather than to meld into a socially expected role, promotes the potential for new experiences to take shape, including the opportunity to build the confidence now that was not encouraged when the client was growing up.

"YOU CAN"

"You can" is one of the central messages I impart to my clients. I have found that this simple idea has not even occurred to many of my gay male clients. "You can" is the underpinning of all clinical work, and yet clients, especially gay men, are taken by surprise when they hear it or feel it. Having grown up rejected or disconnected, the message is incongruent with their experience and the evidence they have gathered to this point. Once seeded by you, experiential work allows clients to internalize this essential message, so that the negative images that were all powerful in the past lose their potency in the present.

SETTING THE STAGE
FOR EXPERIENTIAL WORK

- Be cognizant of your body language with your client; make sure to imply interest in what he is saying and confidence in his being. This may be unfamiliar territory for your client: to have someone be honestly interested in his thoughts, feelings, and experiences.

- Note how he already utilizes his strengths and let him know you recognize this in him. Being seen by you will touch him deeply, and it may help him to recognize some positive new aspects of himself.

- Identify his strengths by pointing them out directly and also highlight how insecurities can be distortions of reality. Insecurity is likely playing a big role, creating a false bravado or tendency to withdraw to allow the client to defend himself and leading to anxiety.

- Use an interactive, engaged approach rather than a laid-back or formal approach (which can be misconstrued by clients as your being disinterested or, even worse, homophobic).

- Recognize authority figures in your own history who saw your talents and encouraged you to excel, and channel them as you encourage your client.

- Accept that your voice is a positive one of authority, perhaps a unique one in the client's life.

- Trust the significance of your role and affirm to yourself that your confidence and beliefs can help him reshape his own beliefs about himself.

THE BENEFITS OF
THE MIND-BODY CONNECTION

I use these terms *experiential work*, *mindfulness*, *relaxation*, *imaginal work*, *guided imagery*, *contemplation*, and *stress management techniques* somewhat interchangeably. Regardless of the term used, the following techniques may be employed in pursuing greater well-being, as they foster more ease and an expanded sense of self:

- Slowing down
- Engaging in calm, deep breathing
- Carefully observing what is happening inside
- Exploring feelings of comfort
- Moving toward an inward focus by shifting attention from external distractions

- Amplifying affirming experiences while diminishing painful ones
- Aligning the mind and the body
- Recognizing and diminishing distorted thinking
- Gaining increased access to sensory and somatic experiences
- Spontaneously eliciting solutions as a result of practice

Keep in mind that even clients who are willing to try mindfulness exercises may be reticent about doing something different than traditional therapy. Remember the gay man's history. Trying something unusual, especially with eyes closed, may trigger conscious or unconscious trust issues. Experiential work may seem scary if your client is thinking that he will be out of control somehow. Some clients are direct about their uncertainty, whereas others imply it in their tone or body posture. Bringing this out into the open may be all that the client needs in order to proceed.

Success in achieving mindfulness will bolster your client's ability to problem solve and generate resourceful decisions. He will begin to trust an inner voice or part of himself that he has routinely neglected. This is a wonderful treatment outcome with ongoing positive potential.

HOW TO INTRODUCE
MINDFULNESS

- **Set an encouraging tone:** Discuss how many clients who try these practices are pleasantly surprised by how peaceful and safe they feel as a result.

- **Reassure the client about safety:** Point out that he will be totally conscious and alert to what is happening the entire time and that you will simply be providing gentle guidance for going inside.

- **Demonstrate confidence in this process:** Provide examples from your personal experience or from other clients. (As one of my clients put it, "I am usually living in two states, zombie and fragile. But this woke me up! I now have a third state, which is alive and able to take care of myself.")

- **Emphasize that the client likely has been successful in using this skill before:** If he has previously done any kind of breathing, centering, or meditative exercises, he has already had a glimpse of the approach. Explain that you will just be showing him ways to understand the benefits and applications more specifically and that your techniques are specially attuned to him.

- **Provide positive details about what to expect:** Highlight feelings of well-being, relaxation, and feeling more in control in the present.

HOME IS WHERE
THE HEART IS

Clients with anxiety or trauma histories may initially be leery of experiential work. It is best to focus on safety and control without pushing them beyond their comfort zone.

Before starting, give a straightforward explanation to frame expectations. If a client is hesitant, then reassure him that is not necessary to use experiential work at this time. Your client gets to be in the driver's seat, and he will trust you more as a result.

Clients with painful histories also may assume that they don't have the ability to do or experience anything positive. They don't yet recognize internal resources. Go slowly and demonstrate patience, building up the client's comfort by trying little pieces at a time. For instance, begin by having a client breathe slowly with his eyes open, practicing this several times and encouraging him with every breath.

Consider consulting with a trauma expert if you don't have adequate training in working with trauma. Your willingness to reach out is an important way to care for and set an example for your clients.

Now more than ever, our lives get so busy and frenetic that at the end of the day we end up feeling both exhausted and empty. What's more, given the digital ecology we inhabit, we are usually connected on one level while simultaneously disconnected on another, and most of us are under ever-increasing pressure in our careers to spend endless hours plugged in, even at home. Mindfulness is by definition unplugged and restorative.

There are additional burdens of being gay that can be alienating. Having to expend more energy to deal with these struggles means less connection, external and internal. As gay acceptance spreads, there has been an unanticipated downside: The number of gay neighborhoods is diminishing. Once a kind of oasis, the gay neighborhood is being dismantled. Thus, opportunities for easy social connection drop away. Far from family, often estranged, gay men may experience a quiet feeling of melancholy. The practice of mindfulness can help our clients reclaim the place of connection inside as they renew feelings of nurturance and self-care.

BEGINNING EXPERIENTIAL SCRIPTS TO USE WITH CLIENTS

Because true happiness comes from inside rather than from others, it is important to align with internal states of being rather than exclusively fighting for external validation. The following scripts will help establish this ground.

For the Body Awareness script, you will encourage your client to really pay attention to what is being said and what he is feeling. Explain that this is a moment he can enjoy by simply being aware of what his body is experiencing in a pleasurable way. Describe the benefit of inviting in a sense of expansion, so different from fragmentation, compartmentalization, and blocking. Developing body awareness allows your client to begin replacing external validation with internal emancipation. Your gentle ability to use the following script will empower the client in ways that may surprise and delight him. You may employ this brief script when your client is unable to generate solutions for himself or is struggling with identifying his own stance.

Before you begin, mirror the client's posture of resting into his chair, with feet on the floor and arms uncrossed. This helps you feel centered, and it lets the client feel accompanied by you rather than being the subject of an exercise. Be alert to whether it is comfortable for him to close his eyes. For men who have trauma in their backgrounds, starting out with eyes closed may set off alarms. It is something he may do naturally as you begin guiding him, but it's important to remember that relaxation is a very tall order for some people, and attunement is always key.

WHAT DO YOU NOTICE IN YOUR BODY?
(BODY AWARENESS)

"You can appreciate what it is that is happening inside of you. You may not be aware that within yourself, within your own body, there are things that you can listen for . . . things that you may not think you know, or things that you would like to know.

Just notice the thoughts you are having in this moment. Excellent."

[Encouragement peppered throughout scripts is important, as clients will generally respond well to recognition and affirmation.]

"Notice images that come to you in this moment . . . like pictures in your mind. You might even notice emotions that you feel or physical sensations inside of your body. Good. Really pay attention to what it is that comes to you. Just be open to whatever these images, thoughts, and sensations are, and it doesn't even matter whether you can make sense of what all of this means . . . we will discuss it in a few moments."

The Body Awareness script is always powerful, particularly with clients who are heavily cognitive. The simple encouragement, just a few focused lines, can begin to guide the client toward the resources needed to empower him to face specific and more general challenges.

As a client is willing to continue the practice of slowing down and being present, he will begin to notice positive changes. The view is different once the client's outlook shifts. A new life pattern may begin to take shape as greater confidence takes root, relaxation deepens, physical health and symptoms improve, and an overall sense of happiness becomes a state of being. He will likely be pleasantly surprised by his own capacity for change. You knew it was there.

The next script, Secure Place, is a great start to ongoing experiential work. Many clients enjoy the tone of voice used and find it reassuring. Learning to use one's voice effectively is a helpful tool. Sometimes the most powerful experience is for our clients to realize that they have the capacity to relax inside. In the case of gay men, who have learned so well the dangers of trusting their body or their instincts, this release can be extremely profound. Subsequent sessions can be paced to add more positive experience little by little.

The Secure Place script (and other variations) is used in several experiential modalities. The purpose is to remind clients that they have the internal resources to create and to maintain a sense of inner security. Following a basic induction, or the Body Awareness script, the Secure Place script may be used and adapted according to the current needs of the client.

Clients may be impressed by their capacity to enjoy the experience. We can remind them that in doing this work they have accessed their own resources. I try not to get too caught up in providing a detailed cognition of what they will experience, since just having the experience is the best way to appreciate its power.

Keep in mind that for gay men, the issue of trust is always front and center. The gay male client needs to be sure he can trust you, and given his history of having to hide from others in order to feel safe and to be accepted, this is understandable. It isn't necessary (or persuasive) to go overboard explaining that you are comfortable with a client who is gay; it is most effective to simply show it—to actually *be* comfortable. Mutual respect will develop quickly and the power of the work will emerge once the container of trust is established.

SECURE PLACE

"And now that you are feeling relaxed, you appreciate how good it feels to be in this place inside. Even if it feels like a long time since you have been in this place, you can appreciate a time in the past, either recent or long ago, when you felt this way.

Perhaps you can remember being in a place in nature, a place while on vacation, or even a really comfortable place inside your home."

[Have the client explore this in depth, as this is where the power of this exercise will come from.]

"If nothing comes to you, you can use this moment here with me as your own special place."

THERAPEUTIC REWARDS

If we feel comfortable being creative and using our intuition to guide us while leading experiential work, we will be rewarded with a natural collaboration with our clients.

Remember the following:

- One's vocabulary is more than words.

- A variety of physical and auditory considerations are available (e.g., a different tone of voice to emphasize an important point, leaning forward to underscore the desire to really hear the client, a quick smile to indicate encouragement, or a deep breath to demonstrate relaxation).

- Your creativity and confidence will grow as you gather affirmative feedback from clients.

- Your clients don't want you to be a blank slate. They want you to be connected and engaging.

- The most effective treatment emerges through customizing sessions for each client rather than using verbatim scripts or formulaic strategies. Customization begins with the first encounters. Attunement begins there. Then, creativity flows in a natural way that feels organic.

- As we allow ourselves to let go—of rigidity, of fear, of our own critical voices—we become less concerned with the perfect intervention and we simultaneously become more attuned to clients' needs. Becoming exquisitely aware of those needs, we open ourselves to incorporating them (utilization) into the specific interventions we use.

- Attainment and customizing deepens a client's experience. Being seen and understood will invoke delight in him. The value of this experience will come to life for him inside your office, and he will bring this to other places in his life.

As we attune to clients' ways of expressing themselves, we can pluck resonant words, images, and sensations that can be used in later sessions. Sharing in the client's vocabulary helps build natural bridges between problem and possibility.

THE PARALLEL PROCESS THAT COMES AS A SURPRISE

As a therapist, you may notice that the thought of using your creativity may bring up some tension. The invitation may be asking you to stretch in ways that you are not accustomed to: Sometimes our background of formal education and pursuing various certifications seems to preclude the idea of creativity. This is actually similar to what many clients feel when we introduce experiential work. Still, we know that when the client is able to find a way to let go of one type of control, to be less constricted and reactive, he feels better. In a similar way, as you deepen your comfort in being creative with your clients, you will feel better too—freer and more invigorated.

Access to creativity begins with allowing what comes to you in the moment to have a place, to be valued first, and then utilized in a positive way. This step really makes a difference in your clinical work, especially with gay men, who, as we have noted, often are not at all comfortable with their own creative spirit. Thus, you are not only finding new ways to communicate and to be mobile in your work, you are also holding up a mirror that reflects ease with yourself and your own kind of artistry. Perhaps your accessing your creativity can allow the client to do this, too.

Change in therapy means movement—an interplay between internal shifts and fresh actions. Trying things he has never tried before, the client can explore what it feels like to trade in hard-and-fast rules of control (protection) for more alive and generative options. You go first.

GETTING IN TOUCH WITH YOUR OWN CREATIVITY AS A THERAPIST

- **Become alert to everyday sensory experiences.** Awakening to the daily happenings around us and archiving them, whether by writing them down or simply really noticing them, is not only nourishing for the creative spirit, it is directly relevant to therapeutic work. You can slow down to take in the images, stories, and metaphors that pop up in your daily life outside of work. Gather them and bring them into your therapy office from which to draw. Working experientially means being quick on your feet, improvisational, and inspired. There is no wasted knowledge!

- **Stay open.** Make sure to communicate receptivity through your posture, the timbre of your voice, and the expressions that move across your face. What you actually say will resonate more when it is backed up by your nonverbal vocabulary.

- **Humor can be a powerful tool.** Learn to effectively use humor (which is different than sarcasm) during a session, keeping the right balance of lightness and seriousness.

- **Take some risks in your work with clients.** You are educated, experienced, skilled—creativity and intuition may prove to be the ingredients that enliven your experience of the work.

"The meeting of two personalities is like the contact of two chemical substances: If there is any reaction, both are transformed."

— Carl Jung

3 Attunement and Authenticity: Utilizing the Therapeutic Relationship to Enhance Outcomes

FIRST THINGS FIRST

All gay men have grown up in a negative ecology, disparaged and denigrated by family members and community members, by media and history. Their feelings are not mirrored by those around them, and so self-understanding is not easily within reach. This experience makes an indelible mark, and its effects can be felt everywhere in adult life, especially when forming new relationships with important others, including healthcare providers.

So, the stakes are high when gay male clients walk through your door. Comfort and compassion are essential components in successful treatment, with the immediate goal being to create a positive alliance. Growth takes root in this alliance regardless of which therapeutic models or specialties you offer.

Because connection takes precedence in this moment, the paperwork that usually is a part of doing a formal assessment (intake) can be put aside in favor of establishing rapport. In this moment, you will choose not to rush through bunches of questions and instead focus on more mindful interactions with your new client. Paperwork can wait, connection cannot.

Gay male clients will be especially sensitive to certain aspects of interaction and particular qualities in you. Gay men are very good at detecting acceptance; they are also exquisitely sensitive to disapproval that is cloaked in formal politeness or "professionalism." In response to the danger posed by much of the world growing up, most gay men have developed a well-attuned radar system.

The following assessment will help you evaluate your readiness to be a genuinely gay-affirmative therapist. Whether you are in the middle of a therapeutic relationship with a gay male client or simply are aware that the next call may be from one, these questions will help orient you to what requires some personal attention for you. **The first set of questions is for the therapist who is working with gay male clients but is not a gay male. The second group is designed for the gay male therapist.**

= Therapist Assessment Form =
Attitudes
(For The Therapist Who is not a Gay Man)

EVALUATE YOUR READINESS:

DIRECTIONS: Simply respond by circling "yes" or "no." Room is provided to elaborate on why you have answered one way or another.

1. Do you understand the unique history that gay men have experienced?

   Yes   No

2. Can you imagine its impact?

   Yes   No

3. Are you able to appreciate a gay male client's issues without judgment?

   Yes   No

4. Do you see your client as a whole person rather than seeing being gay as his identity?

   Yes   No

5. Are you really at ease with gay people?

   Yes   No

6. Can you convey respect and care in your interactions? (If he is coming to therapy with issues pertaining to sex, intimate relationships, or compulsive behaviors, feeling safe will be front and center for him.)

   Yes   No

Elaborate on your answers without editing yourself:

_____

_____

_____

As you further consider what might arise for you, additional questions
may form:

1. Are you comfortable enough with a gay male client for him to feel
    comfortable with you?

    Yes   No

2. Do you convey a sense of professionalism?

    Yes   No

3. Are you secure enough to reach out for additional guidance should you
    need it?

    Yes   No

4. Can you form an alliance with a client who may be cautious in
    pronounced ways based on a history of feeling unsafe?

    Yes   No

Again, elaborate on your responses without editing yourself:

_____

_____

_____

= Therapist Assessment Form =
ATTITUDES
(For The Therapist Who is a Gay Man)

As you work with gay clients, consider some of the issues that may crop up and perhaps surprise you. Try to be as truthful as possible as you think about them.

1. Is there anything you are taking for granted about your gay client with the assumption that because you are also gay, you already know the answer?

   Yes   No

2. Are you the right therapist for this client beyond the fact that you are also gay?

   Yes   No

3. Are there ways that shared experience may actually blind you to certain issues rather than alert you to them?

   Yes   No

Elaborate on your responses without judgment:

_____

_____

_____

All therapists who work with gay clients (and, yes, all therapists in general) need to self-evaluate periodically. Like the musician who tunes the piano, the therapist takes care of his or her instrument, not because it is broken but because it is valuable.

Gay Men are Like any Other Clients—And Not

Your client's needs may cause him to look outside of himself for acceptance, and your job at the beginning is a tough one—and an interesting one. It is easy to fool ourselves by thinking that we are simply kind and open people so that connection is a foregone conclusion. This is a mistake: Paying attention to subtle interactional qualities is crucial to creating a sense of trust. There are developmental stages that both therapist and client go through.

If the client has been in therapy before, his explanation of "I wanted something new" may warrant some exploration. What happened? Did he sense disapproval from the previous therapist? Did they reach a therapy impasse? Was he having trouble translating insight into action? Whatever the reason for having left the previous context, you're his therapist now, and in order to meet him where he is, you will need to appreciate his dilemma, figure out his relational style, and provide the fertile ground for new growth.

Keep in mind that most gay men are used to sitting on the sidelines. Showing sincere enthusiasm is inspiring, although it may take some time for him to adjust to the direct attention. Most clients come to therapy wanting to resolve a problem. Some clients are clear that a good connection is key to good outcome, but others may not be aware of how important this aspect of therapy is. The therapist should be.

A Mindful Moment

Sometimes quick moments outside of the conversation help clients to deepen trust immeasurably—in you and in themselves—as they begin to really be able to discern past triggers and feelings from what is in the here and now. Your continuing attunement and authenticity have more and more meaning as the veil drops. So, again, take a moment, and instruct the client to do the following:

- Gently close his eyes or soften his gaze.
- Allow the comfort that he has already become used to, having practiced with you, to come to him now.
- Appreciate how the sounds of your office create the calm feeling that is connected to previous mindfulness sessions.
- Really hear the tone of your voice as a guide for trust, comfort, and safety.
- Notice how effortlessly he is able to access this simple transformative moment.

ATTUNEMENT

As therapists, most of us appreciate the significance of becoming attuned to our clients, or we wouldn't be working in this field. Three main factors of attunement, 1) using body awareness through experiential work; 2) focusing on clients' resources; and 3) using the strength of the therapy relationship, are integral to fostering change. You and your client will simultaneously enjoy the rewards of using this three-prong approach. You will find out more about these elements of attunement later.

- **Body Awareness:** You can teach your client ways to see that it is possible to reclaim his body as a safe container, able to integrate new information and positive experience.

- **Client Resources:** Regardless of what else your client has or has not achieved, he made it to therapy. Some level of hope, resilience, and strength has gotten him here. Bringing into better focus his resources will have immediate value.

- **Therapeutic Relationship:** This is something that begins to be established immediately. It will be there when good movement is happening, and it will be there when clients feel stuck or angry.

YOUR NATURAL SELF

Whether it's your areas of expertise or good reputation that brought a client to you, acknowledging and appreciating these aspects of yourself adds to the ease of fit. Natural aspects of you, such as warmth and interest, are the currents that pervade the environment, the air that the client will breathe. Being in contact with your natural strengths is good for the environment!

ATTUNEMENT IN ACTION: TIPS FOR BUILDING A STRONG ALLIANCE

As you read the following tips, take a few moments and allow yourself to access your relationship to each one. Perhaps you may consider the entries in a contemplative way, or jot down ideas about which tips you would like to work on, and how. You may think about them in a general way or with regard to specific clients.

- Create an inviting, informal, but professional atmosphere.
- Make eye contact with your clients (even when they cannot hold it).
- Be aware of your body language and show yourself to be open and welcoming.
- Use your intuition to create a relational match by joining the client in his ways of perceiving things and taking in life.
- Trust the unique ways in which information comes to you as you sit with your client. Be confident about utilizing them.
- Use positive humor (not sarcasm) with purpose in order to promote closeness or emphasize a point. Be light and respectful. Note the client's style of humor and how easy or uneasy he is with the use of it.
- Allow connection to emerge organically. You can nourish connection in small ways at every juncture without pushing.

PREPARATION FOR YOUR CLIENT'S VISIT: A THERAPIST SELF-CHECK

As a therapist, you need to prepare to do your work by taking care of yourself before reaching out. Mindfulness in relationship begins with mindful contact with oneself. No matter what happened in the previous interaction (with this or another client), this is a fresh opportunity. Optimism on the part of the therapist sets the right tone for possibility; it is the fertile ground. This means that the session today must be free of the residue of what came before. Even if some unfinished business requires attention, it should be viewed from the present not the past. This is the task of the therapist. Use the Therapist Self Check-In on the following page.

= THERAPIST EXERCISE =
SELF CHECK-IN

DIRECTIONS: Take some time—whether a few minutes or a morning—to let yourself consider and then release feelings from previous interactions. The following list will help guide your self check-in.

- Are there thoughts popping up that have nothing to do with the meeting to come? Let them come in and then be released in this moment to be picked up later if necessary. You may even write them down, so you can literally put them aside.

- Acknowledge any physiological sensations that are with you—muscle tension, constricted breath, headache, jitteriness. Take a moment to use your favorite relaxation approach, from deep breathing to listening to some classical music.

- Note any emotions that seem to be in the background. Call them by name, and send them away for the moment, knowing that you will work through them later. In other words, you will take the time to attend to them but not allow them to inform the next meeting in hidden ways.

- As with the thoughts, sensations, and emotions, acknowledge any images that are with you, and release them in this moment.

- Let yourself gather internal support, just as you guide your clients to; for example, by thinking about the people who respect and care for you.

- Take a moment to center and clear your mind.

- Breathe. Remind yourself of all of the learning you have gathered. Allow your teachers to come to mind. Feel into your care and wisdom and the expansiveness of your heart and mind. Claim all of this as your ground. Breathe.

- Welcome, client.

WHAT DOES IT MEAN
TO BE GAY AFFIRMATIVE?

For gay men, positive experiences with authority figures are few and far between. Most gay men have concealed their identity or behaviors, recognizing the danger in the fact that people in positions of authority might be disapproving, or worse. I still find, for example, that many clients don't tell their physicians they are gay, despite being sexually active. They are afraid the physician will react negatively, and the need for interpersonal harmony surpasses anything else. Of course, it is of the utmost importance for gay men to maintain good physical health, which includes getting regular HIV tests and immunizations for hepatitis and having good information around safe sex. If a physician or therapist is perceived as having a negative judgment, secrecy is the default mode for many gay men. They forget that they have other options (because when they were young, they did not). This scenario happens often in psychotherapy, especially where sex and/or the use of substances are concerned.

I have highlighted that gay male clients flourish through your ability to notice and utilize their own resources. Although it isn't difficult, the idea of enlisting client resources is often neglected amidst the myriad of therapy protocols and emphasis on identifying treatment goals and because clients are well versed in fitting themselves into a model of pathology. Gay liberation itself is still fairly young (since the early 1970s); affirmative therapy for gay males is even younger.

It seems incredible, but before 1990, there was ample literature to support the idea that conversion from homosexual to heterosexual was a useful intervention. Some therapists believed it was in the best interest of their clients, given the common belief that it would be impossible for a gay man to live a happy life or have a stable relationship. You will likely have clients who received this treatment, especially those who grew up in conservative families.

People who come from backgrounds where they were surrounded by positive authority figures may not realize that a gay man has had a history of tending to the needs of authority figures (including parents) in his life by keeping quiet and keeping secrets. This client may recreate in therapy the dynamic he had with his parents by remaining largely hidden. The need to be compliant often prevails. Your challenge is to be on the lookout for such a dynamic and create a tone that implies openness and acceptance. In your therapy, the client can gain a life-altering perspective that is anchored in new experience: moving from an identification with pathology to an alignment with wellness.

THE GAY-AFFIRMATIVE THERAPIST IN ACTION

You want your client to feel comfortable, valuable, and proud. You want to communicate to him that you are in accord with his true self. You can do this by finding avenues of connection with him, as a whole person, not just as a client. (And you must be honest with yourself about your own views and experience. The earlier worksheets are designed to help you with that.)

Allow yourself to appreciate how you respect him, where your commonalities intersect, and how your differences are intriguing. This way of relating is not so much didactic as intuitive. Either you both will feel it, or you won't. There is no need to try too hard to win him over; it is your ease and honesty that are most convincing.

The following script was inspired by a client sharing his difficult experiences of coming out in college. Because these struggles were having an effect on his coursework, his professor asked to meet with him. His memory of receiving support from this professor all those years ago was so profound that he describes it as a turning point in his life. The lamp that was shining on his professor's desk figures prominently in his memory. The visual representation of this lamp still captivates him and represents the richness of this experience, even 30 years later.

I am struck by how other clients report similar types of childhood or young adult memories, often involving positive interactions with neighbors, grandparents, aunts, uncles, or other people who made the effort to express love at critical times.

The Seeing You and Knowing You script can be used as a reminder that there were people in the past whose nurturance made a lifetime of difference. I suggest that you try this script for yourself in order to appreciate the vulnerable feeling of being different and the ways you coped with it. This will help you discern which clients might benefit from the script experience and let you use it with confidence. If a client has suffered trauma and cannot connect with the image of a person, you may bring in the image of a pet, a place, an activity (such as drawing or horseback riding), or even a cherished toy or book.

SEEING YOU AND KNOWING YOU

"Allow a time in your past to come to you when you may have felt awkward, just a little bit different from others, or perhaps you felt alone. It might have been as a child or as a teenager, and you can look back and appreciate what it was like for you then, remembering the ways that you may have held yourself back or constrained yourself. You can even assume that position in your body right now.

You can also appreciate how time has shifted for you now, since you are no longer at that place any more.

Now, remember a person back then who could see you and know you for who you really were and for what you needed at that moment in time. You can appreciate now just how it feels that you knew that he or she cared about you, how lucky you were and are to know that he or she cared. This caring person may not have even verbalized the ways that he or she could appreciate you or the ways that you mattered, but you just knew it was so. You simply knew this by the way the person looked at you, spoke to you, or did something special, just for you. Appreciate the way it feels inside.

It may have been a teacher, a doctor, an aunt, an uncle, or perhaps a neighbor who noticed you and took care of you in just the right ways.

In your mind, you can see what this person looks like, where you were back then, and what the surroundings looked like. You might even remember the sounds or smells of that time. That is right.

In this experience (connection), you could feel who you really were and really are, and it offered you support and an experience of love, and it felt so very special. It was just what you needed. Appreciate how it feels now and assume that position in your body. That is right."

As stated previously, if invoking the memory of a person is not helpful due to trauma, you may invite the client to recall a place, an activity, a pet, a special toy, or a book/painting/piece of music.

Once the script has been completed, you will note what you have tracked in your own experience or what you have seen in the client, including physiological, emotional, or cognitive changes, such as deeper breathing, a decrease in psychomotor agitation, or less triggering around past disappointment or anxiety.

The success you achieve with your clients comes in part from your ability to join them in their world. This often feels like a trance state or state of flow where everything else goes away and it is just the two of you. The ability to join with a client involves putting your own perceptions and experiences aside in favor of respecting his—a task that is sometimes challenging.

The payoff when you can establish comfort with vulnerability is that you and your client together gain greater access into the richness of the client's internal world; this happens through joint exploration and joint experience.

A deep state that is creatively assembled and experienced emerges, for the most part, unconsciously rather than in a planned way. Let spontaneity be your guide, and trust your impulses. The preparation you have done before this (and every) session will serve you well as you easily connect with your skills, creativity, and integrity.

Very often, while doing experiential work with my clients, I am aware that I am talking to the child part of them and that they are responding to me both as children and adults. Thus, I exaggerate the softness or the kindness in my voice during these moments. The client is often nodding his head, receiving my voice—its cadence and tone—as though listening to a lullaby. Inevitably the experience of being understood and appreciated moves clients to tears as they feel a sense of relief in allowing the young part to be truly visible and accepted.

"I AM HERE FOR YOU"

"*I am here for you*" is a stance more than a sentiment.

I actually use the sentence or imply it often and with great sincerity. It cuts through many protective layers when offered at the right moments. Sometimes I directly say it in hypnosis. If a client is struggling with pain, I want him to know that he doesn't have to hold it by himself—that I am not afraid of it and that I will not withdraw when he feels it. This is a hard thing to believe for men who have been denied—and so have denied themselves—the support of others and of love. They may have a tough time believing that others have the capacity to be there for them and that they have that capacity.

CONFLICT: AN ASPECT OF ATTUNEMENT

Dealing with conflict is an aspect of maintaining attunement. Facing conflict rather than avoiding it is actually a way of welcoming more depth and growth potential. It is helpful to ask yourself some questions before a breach in the normal flow occurs.

= THERAPIST SELF-INVENTORY =
CONFLICTUAL SITUATIONS

DIRECTIONS: The statements that follow are designed to help you discern how you deal with confrontation. Answer honestly by circling the "yes" or "no," and then use the space provided to further clarify and/or shift the initial feeling.

1. When you sense that your client is having a struggle with you, do you encourage him to speak about it?

    Yes   No

2. Do you ask him to describe what he needs from you?

    Yes   No

3. Are there times when you avoid these kinds of conversations?

    Yes   No

4. Do you find yourself giving into your fear of confrontation by placating, overreacting or emotionally withdrawing?

    Yes   No

5. Do you have a sense that your client had struggled with an authority figure and has not been able to discuss it?

    Yes   No

Expand here if you need:

_____

_____

_____

Many of us simply prefer to avoid these kinds of discussions and instead stay focused solely on the client's symptoms and presenting problem. In doing this, we miss out on rich moments. Truthfully, we hope that the connection with our client will foster lasting changes, and that our relationship will have significant meaning—and working through the resolution of conflict is a crucial piece of this scenario. It adds tremendously to the therapeutic experience. It may be the first time in the client's experience that an important relationship has weathered a challenge and come out stronger.

A gay client's history with conflict so often employs avoidance as the navigational tool. But in life, conflict is inevitable; now is the client's chance to move through it in a different way. The question is, will you meet him there?

In any relationship, a period of uncertainty usually follows a disagreement. When a client is willing to stay in therapy after a conflict, we want to reassure him (and to know in ourselves) that things can and will be okay again. We know that working through conflict is essential, but regaining equilibrium in its aftermath is also important. This can be healing for both client and therapist. The Calm After the Storm Script can be used by you privately and/or with your client following a conflict.

WHEN THE THERAPY RELATIONSHIP DOESN'T HOLD

If the relationship is at the center of successful therapy, what happens when the relationship doesn't withstand a certain event or interaction? How do you handle clients who leave therapy following a disappointment? How do you cope when clients leave therapy abruptly? Perhaps there was a conflict of which you were not fully aware or a disappointment a client couldn't voice. As mentioned earlier, each new interaction needs to be in the present; thus, every interaction that has already occurred must be completed with no residue being carried forward. The following script helps ensure a clean lens.

The Reclaiming Your Balance script is used to remind therapists that we have our unique abilities to care for our clients in ways that are intimately and mutually experienced. However, when we get stuck in a struggle with our clients, or they with us, we sometimes forget that as therapists we can often make the shift that promotes closeness or good closure when necessary.

The Calm After the Storm

"You can appreciate that when there is a heavy rainstorm, it is loud and intense. As you listen to the sound of the rain beating on the ground or the building in which you are seeking refuge, it seems as though the storm is never going to end. Roads and walkways get flooded, plants get beaten down, and that unsettling feeling inside feels endless. However, there is always a time when the storm abates. You know that from your own life experiences; yet in the midst of it, the waiting feels endless.

Sometimes, summer storms are the most intense. You can watch the sky turning darker and darker, with the winds growing stronger, and then, the rain comes. But, as quickly as it appears, it also passes. Sometimes you can see the sky split between darkness and lightness. You know that the lightness and the sun will reappear, and not only that, you wait for it. That is right.

Appreciate that really calm feeling in your body as the rain stops and you see the sun coming out again. Everything is brighter and quieter, and even the birds start chirping again. Notice the ways in which things shine as the sun reappears. That is right.

When you were a kid or when you were on vacation, you might have even ventured outdoors after the storm to walk around—walking barefoot, feeling the warmth from the earth or pavement on your feet, seeing the mist rise from the ground, and taking in those after-the-rain smells. It feels so quiet and so calm now, so different from just a few moments before. Really appreciate the ways in which your body absorbs the calmness and the quietness. The worst is over; you now feel so quiet inside, with a deep sense of peace inside. Excellent."

Reclaiming Your Balance

"Allow a client with whom you sometimes struggle to come into your awareness. Remind yourself that the love that comes from warmth and acceptance is part of what makes you a very good therapist in your own unique and special ways. That is right. Allow yourself to fully experience this inside now.

Notice the shift that you may experience as you visualize sitting with this person. Feel it inside of yourself, and notice how it may have shifted from the previous client with whom you do not struggle.

In this moment you can really appreciate the ways in which uncertainty is experienced, perhaps by both of you. Be aware of tightness or tension inside and how you may communicate this to your client, even in ways that may not be direct or in ways that aren't even verbalized. That is right.

Sometimes it is hard to acknowledge this, yet this time it may be just a bit easier to appreciate how you, as the unique therapist that you appreciated moments ago, can be available in a new or different way to this client.

Even though it is hard, you can visualize yourself looking or sitting differently with this client. You can take this moment of feeling centered and bring it into the therapy session with this client. That is right.

Something about this moment right now allows you to acknowledge that there may be ways that you can carry yourself differently with your client, and you can even allow yourself to see a slight shift in the session between the two of you, all because you are able to access the strength inside of you to make a shift. And each time you make a shift like this, a change is felt in the relationship between you, even though it may be little by little. Each change creates success; success is ongoing.

As you see and feel this change taking place, just notice the ways in which you look different, feel different, and are different, both inside and outside. Good. You can bring this with you, inside of yourself to future sessions. You can enjoy the ways that you experience love and acceptance, for others and for yourself."

[You may use this script even when the relationship has ended so that the last two paragraphs take this into account in a beneficial way.]

"Something about this moment right now allows you to acknowledge that there may be ways that you can carry yourself differently with your client as you wish him well, and you can even allow yourself to see a slight shift in how you will remember him and how you recall you and him, because you are able to find the strength inside of you to make a shift. And each time you make a shift like this, the change will have a gentle impact moving forward. Each change creates success; success is ongoing.

As you see and feel this change taking place, just notice the ways in which you look different, feel different, and are different, both inside and outside. Good. You can bring this with you, inside of yourself to future sessions. You can enjoy the ways that you experience love and acceptance for others and for yourself."

Sometimes our defenses, needs, or vulnerabilities keep us from finding the right ways to settle difficult moments. It is up to us to discover the paths to achieving resolution. If this is not possible, there is always the option of suggesting another therapist who might be better suited to this particular client. This is not a matter of deciding that the client is "bad" or that you are "bad"; it is a matter of acknowledging a bad fit. Often, verbalizing the truth of a struggle is more helpful than anything else, and being honest about parting ways is healthier than sifting through continual conflict or acting as though everything is fine when you both know it isn't.

Remember that getting consultation or supervision with difficult cases can be very helpful. Just as we imagine ourselves as helping our clients in "difficult cases," we remind ourselves of the same potential.

ATTUNEMENT IS A PROCESS NOT AN ACHIEVEMENT

Attunement is essential to relationships, and relationships are essential to effective therapy. Gay men have learned to be on guard in their interactions with the world, with themselves, and, yes, with you. Gay men have collected a lifetime of evidence showing that trust equals danger. Of course, you are reliable and professional in your work always; when your client is a gay man, it is important to be alert to any ghosts that might be hiding in your own psyche.

THERAPISTS AND CLIENTS: THE FOUR PILLARS OF RELATIONSHIP

1. **HONESTY:** Be truthful about the extent of your experience, no matter how limited, in working with gay clients. Your client will respond to your willingness to tell the truth. It's marks the beginning of trust. It is a part of wisdom.

2. **AUTHENTICITY TRUMPS KNOWLEDGE:** Success in therapy is rooted in meaningful connection. Attention to the relationship is even more important than attention to the particulars of your technique.

3. **BEING YOURSELF:** Gay men are especially sensitized to identifying whether you are who you say you are (e.g., accepting, trustworthy, steady). Deceptiveness equals danger for gay men.

4. **THERAPEUTIC INTERACTING:** Your love and acceptance are the wellspring of his growth and healing. Your interactions need to be rooted in the fertile soil of love and acceptance—everything grows stronger there.

4 | Expanding Healthy Sexual Behavior

GAY MALE SEXUALITY

The topic of gay sexuality piques the interest of many people, and it is an important topic, especially given the misunderstandings or under-understandings among straight people, including straight therapists. I am highlighting the key issues and questions that underly some of the significant themes in working with your clients. Explaining norms in the gay subculture that impact sexual expectations and performance is a good place to begin.

The gay community has stringent expectations. Yes, the gay boy has made it to adulthood, only to find that there's a new club to make him feel excluded or not quite good enough. The widely accepted gay stereotype has specific standards regarding everything from where one should live to how one's body should look, how to dress, and how to behave. Many gay men chase this "A-list" fantasy without realizing the toll it takes on them.

HERE ARE SOME QUESTIONS TO CONSIDER AS YOU WORK WITH YOUR GAY CLIENTS:

- What are the reasons (deep and superficial) that a gay man buys into this stereotypical imagery?
- What is the emotional cost of trying to meet these standards?
- Is he searching for a sense of belonging?
- Is the promise of this new belonging the antidote to historical experiences of loneliness?
- What are other ways (outside of the pursuit of the elusive ideal) that he can achieve a sense of well-being in the community?

THE RANKING OF PHYSICAL APPEARANCE

Despite the reality of how your client actually looks, there's a good chance he doesn't feel good about his physical appearance. He doesn't measure up one way or another. By the time he is an adult, he has already gone through years of shame about not fitting in. Now he has to withstand the same feelings of vulnerability in what is supposedly his community due to its expectations of perfection.

Gay men frequently have a hard time even knowing what they really look like. Your client may view himself as less attractive than he is, heavier than he is, or in some other way have a distorted view. This warped perspective undoubtedly translates into striving endlessly for physical perfection and then feeling the relentless pain of not reaching the goal. This sense of having his efforts constantly thwarted has deep roots for many gay men.

ACCEPTING STEREOTYPES

"I won't look good unless I live at the gym." That's the mantra. Indeed, the gym offers the opportunity to get into shape and to maintain a healthy body, but for gay men, it is also a place where the pressure about appearance and social standing can be very high. Many of your clients will make constant references to the interactions that take place at the gym.

One regular pound equals seven gay pounds. I say that jokingly, but the truth is that feeling self-conscious is the common state for gay men.

Consider using the following questionnaire when you sense that a client has body image issues or body dysmorphia. A client's answers regarding his time at the gym will tell you a lot and perhaps open up some self-reflection for him. Simply circling a choice decreases some charge if there is any. **Remember: A client's access to honest self-reflection will be rooted in feeling aligned and centered.**

A Mindful Moment

Since the exploration of sexuality and body image is uncomfortable and can trigger rigidity or secretiveness, you can use this mindful moment with your client as an opportunity to reinforce his sense of trust in himself and in you. You will see that his defenses will become less relevant and that he will be more at ease with exploring these themes more realistically.

Help your client to:

- Find comfort inside his body by closing his eyes and connecting to a deeper space inside.

- Realize that he can feel anxious on one level while being able to relax himself simultaneously.

- Appreciate that honesty with himself offers great relief and that he is building the necessary foundation to embrace his own insights.

- Realize that your role is to help him explore his positive options and to be a support to him.

- Feel proud that he is and will continue to feel willing to find the healthiest options to coincide with his desire to experience greater well-being.

BODY IMAGE AND THE GYM

DIRECTIONS: On a scale of 1 to 5, with 1 indicating "Definitely Yes" and 5 indicating "Definitely No," please circle your answer to the following questions.

- Do you go due to specific health concerns?　　　1　2　3　4　5

- Do you go to enhance a sense of well-being?　　　1　2　3　4　5

- Do you go because you feel pressured to do so?　　　1　2　3　4　5

- Do you go to socialize?　　　1　2　3　4　5

- Do you feel uneasy if you miss a day—or a week?　　　1　2　3　4　5

- Do you ever overtrain and injure yourself?　　　1　2　3　4　5

- Do you constantly compare yourself to others?　　　1　2　3　4　5

- Are you making up for how you felt growing up?　　　1　2　3　4　5

- Do you feel good about your appearance?　　　1　2　3　4　5

Gay men are responding to the needs of other men, just as heterosexual women so often respond to the requirements of the heterosexual male–dominated culture. Among other things, gay men can get caught in a cycle of sexualizing themselves and striving to remain youthful looking. Even young men describe to me how horrible they feel about the way they look. It is sad to think that a man just 35 years old can feel washed up, while an 80-year-old man may be chasing the 35-year-old version of himself.

Remember your client's personal history: He has been told he is "wrong" by others for most of his life and has learned that it is best to suppress his sense of vulnerability and to try to fit in no matter the cost.

FACEBOOK AND SOCIAL MEDIA: GOODBYE REGIONAL, HELLO WORLDWIDE

With the rise of the Internet, cultural differences have been replaced by global norms. The stereotypes of gay men are no longer regional. Now pressures to be the "perfect" gay man are even more intense, reaching into every pocket of the global community.

It is common for social media sites to come up in conversation in my sessions with clients. Clients so often feel humiliated by what they see on online. The web promotes the illusion of hundreds of "friends"—all fabulous, handsome, successful, worldly, and posting regularly. Thus, an enjoyable pastime easily slips into opportunities for old shame to rise up and for that old friend, self-loathing, to return.

The Internet provides many alluring opportunities. So-called social networking sites and smartphone apps offer galleries of tantalizing pictures, including pornographic images. Everything is at the fingertips of your clients: apps that let them know the locations of other interested men; texts and more pictures that can be forwarded instantly; menus of services of every kind. A customer simply describes what he is looking for, and there it is! It is quick, random, and easy.

The actual possibility of finding Mr. Right becomes more and more elusive as the fantasy Mr. Right—sometimes *dozens* of fantasy Mr. Rights—pop up every time a client clicks *enter* on his keyboard. The search quickly becomes addictive. Mr. Right may live anywhere in the world—or nowhere in the real world. The use of portable devices can easily become compulsive. The digital world is endlessly stimulating and confusing. Since flirtation, vagueness, and deception are often the norm, the state of arousal remains constant and can be stirred up at a moment's notice. Because visiting these sites is considered normal among gay men, the compulsive nature of the sites isn't even questioned.

Another distressing phenomenon related to social media is that gay men don't even need to leave their houses to find what they are looking for. Why bother to get out of your pajamas or even shower when the quest for a man is browser based and just a click away?

These ideas are so entrenched at this point that many gay men just assume that this is the way to go about making connections, and they miss out on more authentic possibilities for interaction as they sequester themselves inside with their sleek machines. Many of my clients sheepishly confess to being online several hours a day, simultaneously surfing various sites. Even when they are away from their computers or phone, they keep their status as "logged on." The cost of being plugged in for a gay man (and for anyone) is missing out on actual connections and the unmistakable chemistry that happens in certain real-life encounters.

EXPANDING INTERNAL REFLECTION

Your challenge is to help your client recognize and enjoy his many internal and external successes—however they are defined. The identification of current strengths and abilities can help balance or compensate for the inadequate feelings being reignited by external standards. Beginning to trust his inner guidance is a huge step for a gay man (as it got him into trouble growing up), and your support, acceptance, and fresh perspective will be very helpful.
Help your client to:

- Understand how and why the pursuit of perfection can be destructive.

- Strike a balance between the desire to keep up appearances and appreciating what matters on a deeper, more essential level.

- Celebrate his deep qualities—those that are inherent in who he is.

- Make realistic decisions in keeping with his age and stage and that make him feel strong and hopeful.

- Shift away from comparing himself to others and toward seeing himself in a more positive way.

The goal of the following script is to help your client appreciate who he really is and what matters most in his life and to acknowledge the positive attributes that define him. The invitation is to embrace his authentic self as a key to empowerment and growth.

FACING FORWARD

"As you are in this space of comfort, you recognize that on this particular day, you are feeling good. You can really appreciate that not every day is a feel-good day. So when these good feelings present themselves, you really enjoy the energy and the spark, like the feeling of sunshine warming you on a clear day. You feel connected to the brightness—you are part of it. That is right.

Sometimes it is funny that for no reason, you find yourself feeling happy. Or, you may notice that during one moment of the day, you may feel tense or overwhelmed, while later, during another moment, something shifts. Your mood is now cheerful, and yes, this a moment of good.

And during such a moment, you may find yourself looking into a mirror. Notice how you really look. This may feel uncomfortable, but look closely. And in this moment of feeling good, you allow yourself to see things about your overall appearance—your face, your body, your essence—that you can feel good about. That is right.

Of course, there are things that you struggle with as you look at yourself, just as everyone does. We all know how hard this can be. Something about this moment though, feeling okay, allows you to see things in yourself that you actually can enjoy. Excellent.

It may be that the essence of who you are comes through to you right now, like the sparkle in your eyes; or a nice, soft smile on your face; or the sincere expression that you easily convey and that so many others recognize in you. You know that people enjoy these traits in you, and right now, you do too. And it is clear—crystal clear—that even without words, the essence of you shines strongly.

You know what your strengths are. That is right. You trust your strength, and you bring your strength with you, wherever you go. You infuse yourself with confidence and comfort, and you have a strong impact on others. It is like having a supportive friend inside of you, whispering in your ear and reminding you of just how good you are. You feel even better about yourself in this moment than you did when you began this exercise. Excellent.

Of course, you know the many accomplishments you have made over the years, and though you may have doubted yourself or how you appear to others, you recognize that you harnessed your strength and achieved success. That is right.

And as you remember to enjoy the memories of your success, the reflection you see in this mirror shines strongly and proudly—your physical self, looking better and better in each moment.

Appreciate the physical sensations inside of yourself—the ways in which you feel good, physically and emotionally. Let the places where these good feelings dwell inside of you take root. That is right. And this image of contentment, of facing inward and enjoying what you see and what you feel, is now a familiar instinct, to be enjoyed in your body, today and every day in your future."

SEX
DON'T ASK, DON'T TELL

If you are not a gay male therapist (or maybe even if you are), know that sex will be a challenging aspect of the therapeutic conversation for you and for your client. Most therapists avoid asking specific questions regarding sexuality in general, not just with gay men. Worrying that your gay client will feel uncomfortable or not feeling at ease in yourself or being sure what to ask makes the conversation even more awkward. Still, it is an important conversation.

Remember that just because something is unspoken doesn't mean all is well. Not bringing up sex often just reinforces that your client has learned to stay hidden. Sex is an area where "hidden" has meant "safety." Even as a gay therapist, I have to prod my clients to discuss sex, and I have to reassure them that it is a normal topic of conversation in the course of treatment.

Your discomfort likely pales in comparison to his. Revealing his sexual practices is one of the most vulnerable experiences he may have in his therapy with you.

What is the purpose of discussing sex anyway? As in other areas in his life, therapy affords an opportunity for self-reflection and honesty with regard to a client's sexuality. To be able to help him identify his own satisfying, healthy sexual practices is a great contribution.

THERAPEUTIC GOALS IN EXPLORING SEXUALITY

- ☐ Help clients become attuned to their healthiest self with regard to sexuality.
- ☐ Explore and support them in their individual preferences.
- ☐ Help them in understanding how their attachment styles impact their communication (or lack of it) pertaining to sexuality and may influence the choices they make regarding sexuality.
- ☐ Encourage healthy self-expression in the sexual realm.
- ☐ Help them develop comfort in discussing sexuality. (Remember, our offices are a laboratory in which skills are developed so they can be used outside of therapy.)

Be honest with yourself. You have some choices. You could decide not to work with a client because you feel unprepared or not educated enough to be helpful, or you could speak honestly with your client about what you know and don't know, to see if he is comfortable working with you. You can also choose to get some of these questions answered by colleagues who specialize in working with sexuality and gay men. Supervision or consultation is always a good idea.

Hearing about a client's sexual adventures, the frequency of his sexual encounters, the risks he is taking with unsafe sex, or his cheating on his partner are just some of the things that may be part of the conversation in sessions. Increasing your own ability to deal with these issues, both internally and externally, is crucial.

There are many reasons why practitioners avoid talking about sex, such as not have proper training for it or being reluctant to ask direct questions for fear of being too intrusive. The following questions can help you begin this important dialogue.

TRENDS IN HEALTHY SEXUALITY

The times are changing. People are now encouraged to be mindful regarding their sexuality and consider it an aspect of good health instead of feeling ashamed of themselves. Sexual health—a holistic combination of physical, emotional, mental, and social well-being—is a current aspiration. Thank heavens folks are now talking about a kind of sexuality that can grow with us, change as we inevitably do, and bring deep satisfaction in myriad ways, and we do not just have to accept what the drug companies are trying to sell us. It is reassuring for clients, and a nice reminder for us, that discussing sex doesn't only need to include shame: It should incorporate a whole host of life-affirming concepts.

Developing sexually includes recognizing and embracing the passages of life. If we think of sexual expression as being flexible and attuned to the stage of life we are in, then we don't have to strive to act and respond as we did when we were kids. This is an invitation to keep growing and learning within the realm of sexuality—as we do in every other realm!

HAVE YOUR CLIENTS EXPLORE AND UPDATE THE FOLLOWING AREAS:

- How do I currently define an open and loving sexual environment?
- This is my body at this age. What does it do better than ever before?
- What do I really enjoy receiving and giving at this time of life?
- Perhaps "sexy" looks and feels different when I really inhabit this moment. Perhaps I am excited by new things—different than what was exciting to me in my teens or 20s.
- At this age, I will communicate what I want and listen to my partner. Together, we can create something amazing.

"Sex positive" is a concept that we as clinicians need to define with our clients in order to best serve them. Sex positive is exemplified by having an active, pleasurable, and emotionally meaningful sexual life. This is in juxtaposition to the default position of judging or labeling sexual behaviors as abnormal or pathological, something all gay men have grown up with.

ARE YOU REALLY SEX POSITIVE?

Becoming conscious of biases increases sexual health. It is important for us to suspend judgment, to affirm sexual pleasure, to understand that sexuality is a basic need. Before therapists can do this in an open and trustworthy way, it is important to explore personal attitudes regarding sex in general and then specifically about gay sex.

QUESTIONS PROVIDERS MUST ASK THEMSELVES BEFORE DISCUSSING SEX WITH CLIENTS

DIRECTIONS: The following questions cannot be answered simply. Each one will require some thought to get beyond how you think you should answer. Being honest with yourself will serve you well as you move into therapeutic relationship with your gay male clients or even as you consider an impasse that you might be feeling now.

- Will you feel comfortable discussing sex with your client, or will you tense up?

  _____

- Do you sometimes feel prudish regarding sex? Do you worry that this will show?

  _____

- Are you able to adapt your language to use the right words with your client—to speak clinically or informally using language that acknowledges his sensitivities?

  _____

- Do you worry about offending him?

  _____

- Do you worry that your own likes and dislikes regarding sex (your comfort zone and what is outside of it) will show up somehow?

  _____

- What are your internal reactions toward gay men in general?

_____

- Do you know if the information you have regarding gay sexuality is accurate?

_____

MORE SPECIFICALLY, THINK ABOUT THE FOLLOWING:

- How will you feel and react when a client is diagnosed with STDs?

_____

- How will you feel and react when a client is diagnosed with HIV?

_____

- What are your attitudes about casual or anonymous sex?

_____

- If your client developed an STD or HIV as a result of an anonymous encounter, would it be especially challenging for you to feel empathy?

_____

- What are your opinions regarding non-monogamous relationships?

_____

_____

_____

_____

_____

SPEAKING ABOUT SEX
WITH GAY CLIENTS

DIRECTIONS: You will ask these questions as you sit with your client. The answers will be telling. If your client appears to want to talk more about something or doesn't want to talk at all, you will follow his lead. The questions will also let the client know that you are okay with the discussion, which should help him relax.

☐ Did your family discuss or avoid discussing sex?

☐ Did you fantasize about boys/men when you were younger?

☐ How did you justify that to yourself?

☐ Where did you begin to use pornography? At what age?

☐ Did you use gay pornography?

   ☐ How did you acquire it?

   ☐ At what age?

   ☐ Did you ever get caught using it?

   ☐ How was the situation handled?

☐ How old were you when you started masturbating?

   ☐ Did you ever get caught masturbating?

   ☐ How was the situation handled?

☐ Were you ever caught having sex with male friends?

   ☐ How old were you?

   ☐ How was the situation handled?

   ☐ How did you feel at the time?

From these questions, a host of issues may come to the surface, including smaller or more significant traumas, acceptance or lack of it around being gay, wounds to self-esteem, family dynamics, and more. Clients tend to answer in rich detail, and pertinent therapy topics will unfold, allowing you to continue to discuss current sexual behaviors from there.

BE VERY SPECIFIC

Very often, clients prefer to generalize their answers when discussing their sexual habits, especially when describing the ways they meet other gay men. "The Internet," is a vague answer that is a catchall, which keeps clients from having to reveal themselves (to you and to themselves). Many of us will simply nod our understanding without asking for more specific information. Again, the richness of relevant details will direct your work. So, provide a nudge toward specificity:

- Which apps do you use?
- Which websites do you visit?

With these types of questions, you imply that clients will answer directly, not vaguely. You won't be surprised to find out that they are on four or five different websites when they are looking for sex, including various apps, which they have running simultaneously. If you aren't specific in your questions, you won't get the answers that will ultimately be beneficial to clients, and you may be implying that you cannot handle the answers.

Think about a different scenario: You are working with a person with a drinking problem, and you ask, "Do you drink too much?" The answer may come back, "No." That doesn't tell you much. If you ask, "How much do you drink per night?" rather than "How much do you drink?" the answer will be more specific. If you go on to ask about the size of the glass, the information will be even more useful. As your clients sense your comfort in asking relevant questions, they will respond with greater openness.

The exact words you use while discussing sex should match your client's style. How people talk about sex is revealing and by paying attention to their language and tone, you will discover how best to communicate with them. Once I have convinced my clients that it is okay to talk about sex, especially in the context of their individual therapy, I mentally note the words they use. Some keep it formal, employing clinical or medical terms, whereas others talk as if they are describing a pornographic scene from a movie. Attuning to their tone and even word choices is an effective way to discuss sex. With one client, it may be most appropriate to use the word *penis*; with another client, *dick* might be appropriate. **Being flexible (and comfortable) is important**.

Sometimes a little nudge from me helps my clients open up more. I frequently remind them of my experience as a therapist: *"You know what? As I sit in this chair, I hear about these kinds of experiences all day long. It feels more awkward for you, of course. I am totally comfortable hearing and talking about sex if or when you feel ready to discuss it."* This type of reflection emphasizes both my ease with the subject and my experience, and clients often will take the risk of speaking openly in response.

In another circumstance, I might say, *"You seem a little uncomfortable. I can't tell if you're uncomfortable about talking about sex in general or if you're worried about how I'll react. I can assure you that I'm completely comfortable—I talk about this stuff all day long."*

This is the arena where your approval compensates greatly for a client's previous painful experiences of being gay. Remember, your caring is infectious, and being able to discuss sex openly while still feeling respected by you and loved by you is healing in and of itself and may be where the greatest growth in esteem may take place in therapy, since the area that caused the most shame is no longer shameful.

WHAT IS NORMAL?

I sometimes think about how difficult it can be for gay men to be honest with themselves regarding who they want to be and how they want to live. How many get caught in the societal net without questioning it? How many end up feeling trapped without realizing they have choices now that they might not have had growing up? In an effort to belong to one community, what is sacrificed? Sexual practices often are affected by social pressures within the gay community. This subculture encourages engaging in frequent sex in a specified way. To question it might be deemed "anti-gay" (which sometimes it is, of course), so instead, people just assume "this is how we do it."

Sex is widely accessible for gay men. What is considered normal in the gay male community can sometimes support unhealthy aspects of sexuality, including denial. It is common for gay men to compartmentalize their behaviors, which mitigates the chances for an honest assessment of sexual practices. The tendency to compartmentalize or shut down may seem mysterious to some, but it is logical in the geography of the past—both the gay man's personal past (so often steeped in shame and confusion) and society's past.

Anonymous sex has its roots in earlier times when married men assumed to be heterosexual would seek male companionship hidden from view. They would cruise the parks and other areas for anonymous sexual encounters with men.

The openness of sexuality in the gay male community causes fear among some gay men for personal reasons, such as internalized homophobia and unresolved feelings about being gay. What's more, many gay men have suffered trauma at the hands of intolerance and thus continue to be triggered by a certain level of openness. Some of my clients avoid dealing with these feelings altogether by not engaging in sex at all. Unfortunately, that choice usually leads to one's self-esteem and confidence becoming eroded over time. Self-imposed celibacy would seem to be in accord with the admonitions from early childhood.

SEX WITH FRIENDS

Sex with friends is an interesting topic for gay men (and an ongoing topic in my psychotherapy sessions, whether individual or group), especially since the division between friends and potential sex partners is more complicated than for heterosexuals. For heterosexuals, it is still not common to be good friends with members of the opposite sex (though this is changing, as younger people are less rigid about their friendships). However, gay men are choosing friends and sexual partners from the same pool. The lines are murky as a result, and tensions often arise about what direction to pursue when two men are close. Should they pursue sex or friendship? How can a gay man recognize the motives of others? If a gay man has a sexual relationship with another guy but the romance or sexual energy fizzles, is it okay to be friends? How does he make this happen? It isn't at all unusual for gay friendships to stem from former sexual partnerships, but it is a hard transition to weather. People who aren't in the gay community often don't get how a friendship flourished from the dying embers of a sexual relationship! All in all, it is a difficult balancing act that poses challenges but has the potential of one of the greatest possible rewards—that of a close friendship.

The comparably liberated sexual atmosphere in gay subculture may see situations in which sex with friends happens, and that's it—end of story. Being sexual for many gay men is a sideline event that doesn't impact the friendship or change the boundaries in any way. It just is a recreational activity that occurs once in a while. Such ease with this boundary may stump heterosexual therapists!

COMMON MYTHS ABOUT GAY SEX AMONG GAY MEN (AND OTHERS)

- Sex should be easy between us because we are two men and presumably like the same thing.
- Gay men don't struggle with erection issues.
- All gay men have anal sex.
- One man is the "top," and one is the "bottom."
- I should perform like a porn star.
- I should look like a porn star.

Remember, a gay man has rarely really befriended his body—it is the source of so much sorrow. Your clients have been brought up in environments (familial, school, religious, media) where gay sexual behavior was seen as bad, gross, funny, or even evil. As a result, sensory experiences within his body were stifled along the way.

In the realm of sexuality, where norms in the subculture are clearly defined in ways that are externally driven and dissuade a sense of individuality, how does one learn to identify sexual preferences and choices based on authentic desire? More likely, gay men will adhere to norms in the community without questioning them. Countless men do what they think they should do as dictated by media and social networking sites. In this tradeoff, there is less room for individuality and more room for inadequacy. I hear this over and over again from my clients. Men feel self-conscious. They constantly apologize for being physically imperfect. Traumatic backgrounds create dissociation, a disconnect between feeling at home in the world and at home in oneself. Vulnerability and discomfort rule. Feeling comfortable sexually requires intentional work, awareness of sensory pleasures, and mindfulness to experience overall comfort.

ARE WE TALKING ABOUT THE SAME THING?

For many people, sex means intercourse. Anything that isn't intercourse "doesn't count." This is frequently the case with gay men as well. In my practice, I have learned that if you use the word *sex* when speaking with clients, you need to be very specific about what you are referring to! The word *sex* by itself is too vague; there's too much room for interpretation. Some very personal definitions may be being applied. Similarly, if clients use the word *sex* in sessions with you, make sure that you ask specifically what they mean. One of my clients only thought of intercourse as being sex, while any other activity—oral sex, kissing, touching—fell into some other the category not called *sex*. I have found that being willing to press clients to clarify how they understand and describe their encounters allows for productive exploration of this topic in psychotherapy. It has also been important for me to be clear in my communication and not just take for granted that what I mean by *sex* is what my client means.

LOOKING FOR LOVE IN ALL THE WRONG PLACES

A common theme among single clients is the search for intimacy and love. Often, the vehicle is sex. Thus, it is important to explore whether my clients are really looking for a long-term relationship or just a hookup. They are different, and the path to them is generally different. I encourage conversation around how my clients are meeting men and what they would like the outcome to be. Looking for an intimate relationship is not the same thing as looking for sex, though many gay men see them as one and the same.

The energy and tone are different when using sex apps designated for hooking up with guys nearby or going to a bathhouse versus meeting a man in a romantic situation or social setting. Many gay men don't agree with me on this, and I have had conversations about it with my clients over the years. Yes, there is always a chance that a romantic connection can be made by what starts out as a hot sexual hookup, but authentic connection beyond the sexual realm is rarely the outcome when the goal is clearly set as something else. You don't generally go to a bar for a milkshake. Thus, it makes sense to talk about pursuing romance as its own category if that is the client's goal instead of lumping everything together into one. It is important—and we can show that it is okay—to make the distinction between a search for romance and a straightforward sexual liaison.

MINDFULNESS: THE KEY TO BEFRIENDING THE BODY

Access to the full spectrum of sexual expression is in part dependent on a friendly connection to one's body. Mindfulness can help gay men befriend their bodies once again. Being in the present fosters connection. Relaxation is a simple, direct, and powerful way to guide gay men to experience great pleasure in the most basic of ways. This work can be done slowly and gently using simple concepts. After a time, you can add more depth to the experience by incorporating metaphors regarding strength or moving forward steadily and with confidence.

Teaching gay male clients how to feel comfortable, how to be patient and relaxed, can be central to their growth regarding sexuality. If the body moves from being a conflicted place, fraught with anxiety, to being a place of comfort and enjoyment, the positive impact on self-image and relationship will be immeasurable.

The transformative aspect of mindfulness helps clients embrace the connection between mind and body to fully appreciate internal responses and make personal decisions regarding healthy sexual behaviors (instead of adhering to community norms). Personal history, pressures within the gay culture, and gender issues may inhibit comfort and ease regarding sexuality. The first thing you can do is to help your client get out of his head and into a place of greater sensory awareness.

RELAXATION AND CENTERING

Your client will be able to calm himself down internally, distancing himself from self-consciousness, worry, or panic, and moving into good connection with himself. In this more open space, he can develop more realistic self-awareness and acceptance of his own individual preferences. External pressure is not immediately internalized once the ability to remain centered takes root. Embracing these experiential moments resets the compass. Your clients will feel relieved.

DEVELOPING THE CAPACITY FOR INTERNAL FOCUS WILL ENABLE YOUR CLIENT TO:

- Be less externally drawn, which typically is more anxiety provoking

- Develop confidence in noticing and welcoming sensate pleasures

- Possess more realistic expectations of what he is able to achieve (regarding self or with others)

- Shift an internal expectation of self from "porn star" to sensual being

- Achieve confidence in decision-making based on healthy choices, wisdom, and internal desire

- Adhere to internal strength in "heat-of-the-moment" situations in which less-healthy choices might easily be made

- Choose sexual partners and behaviors from a stance of more secure attachment

- Allow self-forgiveness and compassion for earlier mistakes

- Prepare for future scenarios using imagery, imaginal "dress rehearsals," and other techniques to envision healthy satisfying sexual scenarios.

The message here is that healthy attunement creates healthier sex. Healthy sexual functioning includes being able to recognize and accept what a person wants and needs and then communicate this comfortably with partners.

The following script is meant to help the client become more familiar with himself—creating access to his unique users manual! We, as therapists, have the opportunity to remind our gay male client that his body is allowed to have particular wants and desires, to know what to do, to know how to care of himself, and to enjoy his own pleasure center of sexuality. For a gay man, this represents a final paradigm shift away from self-consciousness (and sometimes self-hatred) born of the challenges and trauma of growing up gay.

THE BODY KNOWS AND ENJOYS

Start with basic relaxation, and then transition into the following.

"As you are experiencing a greater sense of comfort, acknowledge and appreciate how this feeling is coming from you, inside of yourself. Excellent. You are allowing this moment to be your very own—a private moment of strength and contentment, which only grows stronger during this time. You feel it inside your body. You recognize where this feeling resides inside of you. Wonderful.

There have been times in your life when you weren't sure if you were able to do something well, and you may have felt anxious or worried or had that tight feeling in your chest or belly. Uncertainty was a common feeling for you. Perhaps you even learned how to give in to this feeling and allowed it to take over. Isn't that the case?

However, your body had its own power, deep inside of you. It provided something special to you. It led you to resources that you could use in your own unique way. So when you experienced distress, a part of you came to your own rescue. You were then able to do or achieve what was needed. That is right. One of these moments will gently come into your awareness right now. No need to try too hard to remember one of these times; it will gently come to you. Excellent. (If he appears to be struggling, you can list possibilities that you know of through your conversations to help prompt him.)

Take a few moments and see and enjoy one of these times. You will remember it as if it were happening all over again, right here, right now. Really be aware of what you see, noticing the details with great attention . . . where it was, when it was."

[Continue to elaborate and, if appropriate, ask the client to describe details.]

"You enjoy how this feels inside. You have taken better care of yourself than you have realized, and that feels very good. Excellent.

There are many things that you do automatically, without even thinking about it or noticing it. Your body provides just what you need, effortlessly and automatically. For example, when you ride a bike, you get on the bike, you find your balance, and as you ride along, you use the brakes and you simultaneously steer the bike. Perhaps it took you a while to build up this confidence, but once you did, you no longer had to worry about doing all of these things at once. Your own coordination became effortless and automatic, without even having to think about it.

The same thing is true with driving a car and many other things you do in each and every ordinary moment of day-to-day life. You choose the right clothing for yourself depending on the weather outside, in various levels of thickness or comfort, based on the elements. If it is warm outside, you pick a light layer or decide that you don't need an extra layer at all, while if it is cool outside, you wear a heavy-enough layer or bring along another layer just in case.

You do all of these things without even thinking about it—you do it instantaneously. You listen to what you need, and you take care of yourself, free of worrying—you just do these things.

This happens in other domains as well. Without noticing, you have taken care of your needs in just the right ways. That is right. From this moment on, instead of worrying, you will find yourself embracing your body, enjoying all that you can do, physically, romantically, and sexually.

Notice the connections you feel in this moment right now. Yes, there is a way in which your body brings you all sorts of nice things—comfort, well-being, or stillness without effort. You can just be in the present and not have to try, not have to worry. That is right, just enjoy.

In other instances, tension or uneasiness and fear may come along. Notice how your body tightens. What is your body telling you in moments like this? How can you appreciate that you can be respectful toward yourself or easy on yourself? Does your mind fill itself with expectations that get in your way? Or can you simply use tools for letting go and experience comfort all over again, just as you have been doing this whole time?

Return to the really good sensations you were feeling a few moments back and notice how quickly you can return to relief. Excellent.

It feels good to feel good. You can take all the time you need, over and over again, to focus on good, pleasurable sensations inside of your body.

There are so many simple ways to be attuned to your own sensations inside, and it is nice to remember that you can, and will, continue to do this.

In this comfortable place, you enjoy a variety of feelings and sensations. When your body tells you what it needs, you listen, free of worry. Your ease in listening will help you to feel more comfortable with messages that your body sends you. As you affirm that your own internal knowing of what you want and need is all right and you enjoy what feels best for you, a smooth feeling of relief washes over you. That is right. Whether it is you allowing yourself to enjoy these moments or you being able to ask others to help you attain this, you will feel proud in your ability to give to yourself from this moment on. Excellent.

This experience will stay with you, in your memory, and in your body. You will be reminded, over and over again, that inside of you is the place where awareness, success, and good feelings will continue to arise. That is right!"

Sex is More Complicated than it Appears

ARE ALL GAY RELATIONSHIPS OPEN?

Open relationships—relationships that are non-monogamous—are not uncommon for gay men. Like many other modes of sexuality in the gay community, this one is easily accepted without people assessing whether it suits their needs or whether their relationship has the strength to sustain being open. Over the years, I have heard many of my clients say that all gay men cheat on their partners. This simply is not true. Those who don't believe monogamous relationships work may have bought into this stereotype without questioning or looking deeper. There are many couples that maintain monogamy based on choice and their particular needs.

Monogamy and non-monogamy are options for gay couples. The latter option does not carry the same stigma that it does in the mainstream heterosexual community.

Unfortunately, many couples don't assess the strength of their relationship before making the decision to switch to an open relationship, or many switch during problematic times hoping it will help somehow, but this is usually a recipe for disaster: Making this transition isn't the way to ameliorate relational or communication problems.

Opening up a relationship can be challenging and rocky. Some decide to pursue an open relationship in order to avoid confronting the challenging problems that exist in the relationship. But this decision really never strengthens a vulnerable relationship; having an open relationship can only really work if the relationship is already strong.

WHAT AN OPEN RELATIONSHIP LOOKS LIKE

In order for an open relationship to work well, there are a few principles that I suggest couples abide by. Agreements are made regarding what is acceptable to each partner (such as the primary relationship comes first, sex outside is secondary), and both partners agree to wanting to open up their relationship rather than one person strong-arming the other into it. A stable couple is more likely to endure a change in flexibility than a couple in crisis.

This being said, it isn't unusual that couples go about opening up their relationship in their own ways that are different from what I suggest here. It will feel a bit scary to you, the therapist; my tips may help.

As I define *open relationships*, my assumption is that we are talking about couples who want to maintain their relationship as primary and ideally, couples who want to continue being sexual. There are many types of open relationships, and I am only presenting one model here.

In providing tips for therapists working with gay male clients around open relationships, I am not suggesting that every couple ought to have an open relationship or that your clients will be able to adapt easily. I advocate for exploration and open communication about making changes in the frame of the intimate relationship.

WHEN SEX IS A PROBLEM

Gay men so often become adept at compartmentalization—a way to defend against shame—and this "skill" is apt to be strongest in the sexual realm, since shame has been most often associated with this domain. As I previously mentioned, gay men are quick to assume that a norm in their community is acceptable without even questioning its impact on them. Therefore, out-of-control sexual behaviors are not uncommon.

There has been a positive shift in terminology regarding sex. Rather than using a disease model or a diagnostic label, like *sex addiction* or *sexual compulsivity*, the term *out-of-control sexual behavior* implies personal distress and a motivation to change behaviors. Not only is it less pathology oriented, it also helps therapists to view our clients' behaviors within a more empowering and less judgmental framework. (Douglas Braun Harvey and Michael Vigorito's book, *Treating Out of Control Sexual Behavior*, is an invaluable resource for your library.)

How do you decide if a client's sexual behavior is healthy, taking into account the norms of the gay community, or whether his behavior is unhealthy? If you are not a gay therapist, you may think that his behaviors are out of control. If you are a gay therapist, you may not. Neither perspective is ever going to be entirely right across the board. The question warrants careful self-exploration prior to responding to the client.

THE HEALTHY LINE

In exploring sexuality with clients, it is important to appreciate the line between healthy sexuality and out-of-control sex on an individual basis. How much time is your client spending in the pursuit of sex? Has he become detached from arts, sports, or other forms of creative expression in which he was once interested? Is he tired, late to work, or does he take extended time out of the workday to pursue sex? Does he turn down meaningful social interactions in the hope that he will find a satisfying sexual encounter?

When a person is caught in the struggle of out-of-control sex, excessive masturbation, or pornography use, he is caught in a state of intensity—anything but a mindful state. He is in his own trance state in which all of his internal focus is on the pursuit. In this trance state, everything else recedes. His focus is on that one thing, and whether it's a computer, an app, an actual person, or masturbation, his internal state is revved up. First, you can help him assess whether this happens to him, and if so, how and when. Then, you can redirect him back to a comfortable position of "mindful self" in order to restore and maintain equilibrium. You will notice the difference in his demeanor, and he will be grateful to you for guiding him to this place of calm and centeredness.

Checking in with Your Own Feelings

DIRECTIONS: The following questions are designed to help you catch emotional reactivity before it catches you. Answer honestly now so that you can handle the issue before brining into the therapy room.

DO YOU:

- Find yourself caught in the bind of advising your client rather than helping him figure out what is best for him? (Keep in mind that advice can feel like disapproval, particularly around sexuality.)

    Yes   No

- Find it difficult to hear details about your client's sexual adventures and as a result, feel uncertain about how to intervene?

    Yes   No

- Feel captivated or even excited by your client's experiences?

    Yes   No

- Feel enraged by poor decisions your client has made or by him putting himself or others at risk when pursuing sex?

    Yes   No

- Find it nearly impossible to hear or discuss anything else except the behavior about which you are most concerned?

    Yes   No

- Worry so much about sounding judgmental or narrow minded and shaming that you feel paralyzed when it comes to intervention?

    Yes   No

If you answered "yes" to some of these questions, take a few moments and let yourself pause to identify your feelings but not judge them. Regroup. Breathe and use your own visualization and relaxation techniques to center yourself. You might think of a colleague to contact for support. Do this as often as you need. Remember, your primary goal in helping your client is to assess whether his sexual behavior is out of control. Your role is to help elicit self-reflection and honesty so he can assess what he is comfortable addressing on his own. If he hasn't been as thorough as you would like, you can ask him if there is something more that might benefit from exploration: "Did I miss anything?" "Is there something you would like to add?" "Do you feel as though I understand what you have said?" These types of questions are powerful at the close of a session because you are inviting more of him to come forward rather than instructing him on what to do.

Remember, it is not your job to police your client's behavior.

WHAT DOES YOUR BODY HAVE TO SAY?

Inviting your client to listen to his body's messages sounds basic, but perhaps you haven't thought to actually try it. Instead of worrying about how you will approach a client with your concerns or fearing that you will pounce on him and lecture him in judgmental ways—instead of being anxious about how you might act or appear—you can re-orient your client to himself. Shifting him away from focusing on the external to focusing on what he is aware of inside is often an effective way to address sensitive questions. This process enables you to guide him to self-reflection without having to confront him. A client may feel defensive when asked directly to assess his own behaviors, but simply inviting him to notice what his body is communicating is a valuable therapeutic tool. You can encourage him to listen to his body by noticing physical sensations, emotional reactions, thoughts that pop up, images that appear, or even sounds he hears. Ask him to appreciate any of his senses and allow himself to postulate in a gentle way about what his body is telling him. If he freezes and is too tense to be able to use this, do a basic relaxation to help him feel comfortable and safe.

If your client can feel safe and begin to track his own feelings, there is a better chance that he can make healthy decisions regarding sexual behaviors. Reactivity—rooted in fear, anger, desperation, or some combination—leads to actions that are often out of touch with what might actually bring your client happiness.

You can encourage your client to decipher his feelings and experiences before, during, or after his sexual encounters. You invite him to explore this in detail and do your best to be free of judgment so he has the necessary space to come to his own conclusions. Guiding a client to differentiate among feelings in the "before," in the "during," and in the "after" can be very profound. Most of us tend to throw everything into one pot, making it difficult to listen for preventative clues or moments when we might make another choice. Having your client pay attention to and acknowledge the state that is giving him information at various times can help him interrupt old patterns. Clients who are comfortable with experiential work are apt to be less guarded and more honest as they explore the questions they ask of themselves. They are invited to wonder rather than be suspicious and are more likely to be able to wonder if you are able to as well.

The following questions invite your client to slow down and experience his own discernment regarding sexual behaviors, including identifying potentially out-of-control behaviors.

Listening to Your Body

DIRECTIONS: Start out using a basic relaxation exercise with your client and then ask the following questions about a specific recent sexual experience. It may not be necessary to break down the before, during, and after timeframes, as the questions are the same for each one, but this format does provide space for clients to really feel into their own sensations apart from external pressures. (Though I use the word *sex*, this exercise can also be used for any sexual behaviors such as using pornography, apps, websites, or masturbation.) Write down his responses in the space provided.

Questions Regarding His Feelings Before Sex

• What were you thinking about beforehand?

_____

• What did you notice was going on inside you during this time?

_____

• What physical sensations were you aware of?

_____

• What emotions were you aware of?

_____

• What were your thoughts about your potential actions?

_____

Questions Regarding His Feelings During Sex

• What were you thinking about during this time?

_____

- What did you notice inside your body during this time?

  _____

- What physical sensations were you aware of?

  _____

- What emotions were you aware of?

  _____

- What were your thoughts about your (potential) actions?

  _____

(Be attentive to any differences in the answers between "before" and "during.")

Questions Regarding His Feelings After Sex

- What were you thinking about afterward?

  _____

- What did you notice inside your body at this point?

  _____

- What physical sensations were you aware of?

  _____

- What emotions were you aware of?

  _____

- What were your thoughts about your actions?

  _____

Honest acknowledgment helps foster the possibility of creating and adhering to healthier behaviors based on self-reflection. Powerful insights frequently arise spontaneously. You will feel good about intervening in this way, and your client will be grateful, as your relationship will also strengthen. Open exploration instead of judgment or advice is a far more effective intervention.

It is difficult to discuss out-of-control sexual behavior with clients; it is hard not to sound judgmental or overly parental. I can attest. I sometimes call myself Mr. Fix-It. When my clients engage in risky sex, my stance sometimes becomes more authoritative than casual, and I take it on myself to "fix" things. My inclination is to advise and feel frustrated if my clients make choices that pose a danger to them or others. In these moments, when I have lost my center, I need to reorient myself in a mindful way.

EGO STATE WORK

If your client is unwilling to acknowledge his struggles regarding sexuality or acknowledges them but doesn't understand them, "parts work" is one of the most powerful ways to help him. Sometimes clients wish that they could just erase the parts (self states) of themselves that don't function as well; for instance, the parts that are out of control. It is important to guide our clients away from wishful thinking while also validating their dilemma. We can explain and then show that it is healthier to recognize that no one part defines a person and that once he makes room for all of his parts, he will find the relief he is looking for. All parts need to be heard, and ignoring or neglecting any one aspect can sometimes amplify its need. Creating the space and taking time to hear from all of the parts is essential.

In this process, clients are able to illuminate how and why all the parts are present—those that are functional and the others that are less so. Eventually, the more functional parts can be called on to help the less functional parts. Parts work, or ego-state work, is a powerful, practical process to use in therapy, especially when it comes to sexuality. It helps motivate clients to compartmentalize less while also appreciating deeper internal motivations that may be healthier.

We intervene by exploring the various parts that propel our clients. Every client who feels out of control sexually has parts that don't necessarily want to act on the feelings that lead him there. We can help him to appreciate these parts and use them for maintaining strength and control. We can help the client explore the weaker parts so he can understand what motivates his less-healthy choices. As his healthier parts become aligned to lead him back to strength, there always is competition between healthy and less-healthy parts. By allowing this conflict to surface, we can guide the client to find ways to reconcile the struggle through strategies that bolster the healthier impulses.

As your client begins to delineate these parts, he will begin to experience greater reassurance, less overwhelm, and a way to organize internal struggles. Ultimately, parts work is one of the best tools there is for understanding and changing behaviors related to sex. It is so quick and powerful that it seems like magic. It isn't, of course, but it is great work! In fact, it is my preferred approach with sexual behavior.

Parts work is useful for the therapist, too. When you use parts work to help your client explore his own sexuality, it is comforting to know that just a part of him is operating. With the awareness that more functional parts are also within his repertoire, this difficult work is less overwhelming. Additionally, if we feel stuck when we are with a client, we can explore within ourselves which parts are becoming activated and how we can elicit other useful parts within us to regain our balance.

I say that the best way to do parts work is to do it your own way, using your own intuition and creativity as guides. My script suggestions are exactly that, suggestions. Translating them into your own language will provide the personal touch necessary to be most effective with your clients.

This following excerpt introduces one way to help the client organize and keep track of his various parts. Each part contains its own distinct sensory sensations. Being able to make space for all parts will be a relief. As a therapist, you will be able to more easily intervene with curiosity rather than judgment.

An example:

- "You say that you enjoy anal sex without a condom and that it excites you. What would you call this part of yourself?" [He answers, "The dark part."]

- Using the client's language: "You refer to your dark side—can we call this your dark side or your dark part?"

- "You also say that you are spending hours checking apps, looking to meet guys. What would you call this part?" [He answers, "The naughty part."]

- "And you also say that integration is missing and that you wanted to stop having unsafe anal intercourse. What would you call this part?" [He answers, "My integrated part."]

- "Are there other parts you are aware of?"

I then focused on each part the client mentioned and asked him to explore his sensory awareness with each one. I asked him to appreciate experiencing these parts by seeing and understanding them as parts of a greater whole, as if they were a family living inside of him. I always take my time exploring the depths of each part and then ask the client to have all parts join together to explore whether there is more for him to learn.

Identifying the Parts

DIRECTIONS: Starting with a basic induction and deepening, you can help the client to identify his parts by repeating his words.

1. "You were saying that you [_____]. What would you call this part of you?" [Encourage the client to use his creativity and put it in his own words in a way that is clear and concise.] Or, "Can you identify what this part is in just a word or two?"

2. "You also said that you [_____]. What would you call this part?" Or, "What would you call the part of you that [_____]?" [Continue this until you have covered all of your client's considerations or until he doesn't imagine any other parts.]

3. "There might be more—does anything else come to you?" [I write each of these parts down so I can remember them; it also shows that I take the parts seriously.]

4. "Just focus on each of these parts separately. Notice what comes to you—what you feel (with regard to this part); what thoughts are in your awareness; what is happening physically inside your body in this moment—images or even sounds that come into your awareness." [The more you emphasize the sensory experiences, the more detailed the answers will be.]

5. "Now, describe what it feels like having all these parts together, hearing each other. Describe what you are aware of in this moment. Does one part want to say anything to another part?" Or, "What do you see? What do you feel?" [I refer to this as big picture awareness, where clients can step back and see the totality of parts in a larger context rather than just singularly.]

A HEALTHIER TRANCE STATE

Since sensory awareness heightens a healthier state of thinking and being, consider maximizing your use of experiential work. In the domain of experiential work, a frequent goal is to help clients develop the ability to shift states. With out-of-control sexual behavior eliciting a potentially negative trance state, we want to provide our clients with an experience that will remind them that they also can easily access a more positive state. The client has all sorts of options to consider. Know that the client will remember—whether it be through conscious or unconscious memory—his ability to experience pleasure. Perhaps he will even choose healthier behaviors as an alternative in the future. Inducing a healthier trance state simply involves having the client recall activities or experiences that bring him joy and increase the sensory volume on an experiential level. The imaginal process kicks into high gear, and he instantaneously is able to achieve pleasure internally, in the healthiest of ways.

The key to success it to know what activities or hobbies bring him the greatest pleasure and amplify the experience as part of the exercise. Allow your creativity and intuition, as well as your enthusiasm, to flourish, which will be contagious! An additional goal is to help the client notice the contrast between healthy and less-healthy distractions in order to provide an opportunity to experience the contrast between these states and then choose what is best for him. The following script is a good tool to use in helping the client experience a healthy trance state.

Healthy Sexuality is a Discovery, Not a Doctrine

Maintaining care and respect for your client can be difficult, especially when his behavior goes against your personal morality or endangers him or others. At the same time, care and respect are key ingredients in all treatment success, especially where sex is involved.

Combining the various approaches outlined in this chapter can create enough positive regard for healthy change to happen. Remember, mindful action and response will take root in true self-care, which means the self is of value; this may be is a new feeling for your client that needs to be supported in mulitiple ways.

Ask for help when you need it. Get consultation or send your clients for outside guidance when appropriate. The insights that come from inside the client are preferable to the advice that comes from you; they have the best chance of initiating the kind of healthy change that can then be maintained and expanded on.

YOUR OWN PERSONAL OASIS

Start with a basic relaxation, beginning here:

"Remember a moment in your past when you were able to shift your focus away from stress or discomfort in a healthy way that you knew was good for you. Excellent."

[If you prefer, you can mention a specific activity that you know your client has enjoyed.]

"This may have been an activity or even a place. Yes! It feels good to shift this focus just for yourself, right here, right now. That is right.

Experience what has come to you, such as thoughts, images, or sensations. Appreciate the ways that you now feel as you remember this moment. Your body and mind feel healthy; you feel good."

[You can ask the client what he has come up with as far as thoughts, images, or sensations.]

Now use your own creativity. Amplify the experience by asking your client to be aware of the sounds or the sensations he experiences. Some examples: If he loves running, ask him to hear the sound of his sneakers hitting the pavement and really appreciate how it energizes him. If he enjoys photography, ask him to feel the weight of the camera in his hand or feel energized by the click of the shutter. If he is a bike rider, ask him to notice the breeze on his face. Whatever the activity, stress the joy of sounds and smells or the magical feeling inside that it sparks.

Shifting Focus

"Now, you can change the scene and allow yourself to notice distractions or behaviors that you know really aren't the best ones for you. You and I both know that everybody has these."

[You can even give examples of other people who make choices that are problematic for them. You can ask the client about what he has come up with if you think it will be helpful.]

"Notice what you feel inside now, such as the thoughts, images, or sensations you are aware of. That's right.

You can acknowledge whatever painful feelings emerge, and you can really appreciate your own ability to be honest with yourself. Excellent. I wonder if your ability to be honest with yourself feels like a relief?"

[Ask him to report what he experiences if you are curious, or imagine that you bearing witness will be beneficial to him.]

Shifting Focus Back to the First State

"I wonder if you can bring yourself back to the first activity that you chose [name it to personalize], the place you can bring yourself to that is far from stress, in pleasurable or healthy ways. Notice what you feel inside now! Excellent.

Once again, just experience what has come to you, such as thoughts, images, or sensations. Appreciate the ways that you feel.

I wonder if there is a way in which your body feels more relaxed. Notice the relief. That's right.

Appreciate the ways in which it feels different to engage in these different kinds of escapes, some healthy, others not quite as healthy. Good.

You know that you can use our own strength, your own abilities, to find healthy distractions for yourself whenever you want, whenever you need."

Typically, clients will report a feeling of relief and will be struck by the activities or internal states that emerge from being or feeling in control. Yes, the difference between these states is powerful, and your client will most likely share details about the experience with great relief.

5 HIV/AIDS: Living with It, Not Defined by It

HIV/AIDS? Isn't it a thing of the past? Isn't AIDS just a chronic illness now, something managed with medication?

It's true that the prognosis for those with AIDS has greatly improved. Still, the history and trauma that gay men and their families, friends, and healthcare providers have endured is inconceivable. The consequences are very much embedded in the present. Furthermore, the disease is far from eradicated. In fact, although AIDS is now more treatable than in the 1980s or 90s, younger men (30 years old and younger), especially gay men of color, are experiencing a serious rise in seroconversion (when sero status is converting from being HIV antibody negative to HIV antibody positive).

This chapter covers many important factors regarding HIV/AIDS, things that contemporary therapists need to know. I provide updated information about HIV/AIDS, past and present, including its impact and current course. The power of mindfulness exercises will be demonstrated for prevention, for helping newly diagnosed clients cope, and for facing the deep grief that continues to move through the gay community as assuredly as survival guilt, anger, and denial.

YOU AND **HIV/AIDS**

Clients who lived through the early days of the AIDS epidemic or have been recently diagnosed as HIV positive need understanding and support, something that is difficult for them to receive even now. Although the conversation has become more open, we continue to be uncomfortable around most illness and especially around illness that carries stigma. So, in this moment you are the one on which he is relying. Will you step forward?

The way in which AIDS has been erased from memory reinforces the lonely, secretive existence that gay men know so well from the past. Perhaps for some forgetting is easier than remembering. At least, that's the feeling on one level.

You can't tell who is HIV positive and who isn't. Thirty-five years ago, when gay men were sick and dying of AIDS fairly quickly, they were so gaunt and weak and the medications produced lipodystrophy or other unpleasant side effects that it was fairly easy to identify who had AIDS. Now it imperative that your client's sexual choices always be made with the assumption that a sexual partner could be HIV positive.

As a therapist, you cannot assume or guess either. You will need to ask clients about HIV testing and their status instead of basing your knowledge on how they look. Some will be ashamed to share their status with you, particularly if you are not gay, and will be more likely to speak frankly if you are direct in your inquiry. Direct, caring inquiry imparts an accepting position, neither avoidant nor judging.

WHAT DO YOU REALLY THINK?

The following questions are designed for the therapist's self-inquiry. Though they may be difficult to answer honestly (as nobody likes to admit stereotyping), you may find it is possible if you take a few moments to find a comfortable internal space. What's more, you may find that a frank assessment brings relief (just as you teach your clients). These questions are not meant to be shaming; rather, they are intended to help you clarify the reactions that most clinicians are uncomfortable acknowledging, to either themselves or others. Take time to mull over the questions, and jot down your ideas if that is helpful.

= THERAPIST ASSESSMENT FORM =

HIV VALUES

DIRECTIONS: Answer these questions in a straight forward way. Self-awareness now will prevent you from being ambushed by hidden feelings later. Most of the questions will require a few sentences, but let your first answer (before embellishment or an attempt to polish) have a place. Nobody else is looking, and this is a chance to be honest with yourself.

- Have you worked with HIV-positive clients before?

  _____

- How do you feel about somebody who acquires a disease as a result of sexual contact?

  _____

- How do you feel about someone who is diagnosed with AIDS, knowing that he was aware of the risks?

  _____

- How do your thoughts about someone diagnosed with cancer differ from thoughts about someone diagnosed with AIDS?

  _____

- If you have worked with a client with AIDS, how have you judged him differently from others clients?

  _____

- Have you wanted to spend extra time, beyond what is really necessary, exploring how your client contracted HIV?

  _____

- How would you feel toward a client who is engaging in intercourse without the use of condoms only to learn that he is HIV positive?

  _____

- Have you yourself ever engaged in any kind of risky sexual behavior about which you felt uncomfortable?

  _____

These are difficult questions. Many people struggle to answer them without distorting their views and attitudes, in essence lying to themselves. Looking deeper into and exploring your judgments will be beneficial to you as a clinician in general and specifically when it comes to sex and HIV/AIDS. Knowing your limitations and understanding them makes it easier to assume a clearer stance and provide more effective interventions with clients. Again, a close relational bond creates success in treatment, and this very much is at the fore when we are considering such delicate and charged themes.

If you know what you are dealing with internally, you have options when HIV/AIDS (or any area with which you are uncomfortable) is part of what is being brought into the therapy. You can choose to refer your client to another practitioner if you find that your biases are challenging. Or you can continue to treat your client while also sending him for consultation with a gay male therapist or provider who has extensive experience with HIV/AIDS issues. If you opt for this, simply normalizing it as good clinical practice will feel comforting to your client. He has a team. You may also choose to acknowledge that you do not have expertise in working with HIV/AIDS so that the client can decide whether working with you is best for him. Options and openness are your friends—and his.

IS IT OKAY TO ASK ABOUT YOUR GAY MALE CLIENT'S SEX LIFE?

The answer is yes—with respect. Gay men hide. Compartmentalization regarding risky sexual behaviors is an unconscious reality for many gay men. Not divulging the truth about risky behaviors or HIV status isn't at all unusual. If you don't ask, they may not tell, often without even realizing that they are withholding information.

You will want to be thorough in asking about sexual history, sexual behaviors, and levels of risk in which your client has engaged. The therapist should imply that the client has been involved in what is being discussed, thereby normalizing it, rather than making the conversation more stressful. You need to probe carefully and respectfully. For example, you can offer a simple statement, such as, "Many of my clients have discussed how they have engaged in risky sexual behaviors. I hope you are willing to do the same with me, as I am comfortable discussing this with you." Be open to hearing the truth, and be patient. You will want to regulate your external reactions just as you have with other tricky clinical issues. This doesn't mean hiding, by the way. It means doing the preparation and assessment outline earlier and then being in alignment in your facial expressions, body movements, tone of voice, and other expressions. Most of us have developed habitual physical tics that show disapproval—a raised eyebrow, curled lip, head tilt. We may not notice it, but the client will. Mindful attention to fully respectful alignment is very powerful. We want to let our care reach our clients in every possible way.

It is common for gay clients not to mention to their heterosexual therapists that they have AIDS, especially if the presenting problem is unrelated and the condition is manageable. They may have been shamed by a provider or doctor before and find it easier to leave out details rather than face the risk of rejection again. It is equally common to leave out details of the sexual behaviors that may be putting them at risk. They will probably assume that you will not understand. I hope that you do the work necessary to developing understanding. Not having to compartmentalize in therapy is central to what makes this setting therapeutic.

PATIENT DISCRIMINATION

Discrimination still exists. It may come from a primary care physician or a specialist in something other than HIV/AIDS who is homophobic, biased, or dangerously misinformed. Unfortunately, many of my clients have shared experiences of being treated dismissively or in overtly homophobic ways by medical professionals. Sadly, this doesn't only occur in areas with small gay populations—I have heard stories from patients in Boston and New York City—but it may be more prevalent in nonurban environments because of a lack of experience with HIV/AIDS, which may engender greater prejudice. Consider asking your clients about how their physicians treat them regarding sex and HIV/AIDS. The resulting discussion may be helpful in many ways.

HIV/AIDS—A QUICK HISTORY

For those who lived through the worst of HIV/AIDS in the 1980s and '90s, the scars remain. Very few gay men were untouched by illness and death. Friends, partners, colleagues, family members—so many were sick; so many were dying. No gay man emerged from those decades unscathed. The trauma of the epidemic was nested in a mainstream culture filled with suspicion and steeped in the belief, overt or covert, that illness was somehow punishment for unnatural behavior and relationships.

Over time, breakthroughs in medications and treatment protocols have allowed people with AIDS to live healthier and longer. For many, the pain of the epidemic has been buried somewhere in history, but of course the memories live on, often hidden from view. For younger men, there is not the same heaviness around HIV/AIDS, although HIV/AIDS is part of their backdrop whether or not they recognize it.

The ways in which HIV/AIDS affected the gay male community are profound and enduring; we wouldn't be where we are or who we are if HIV didn't exist. The AIDS epidemic radically influenced the essence of the gay male community. Even though the landscape of HIV/AIDS has drastically shifted over the years, its experiential impact needs to be acknowledged. Amnesia cannot teach us anything.

SOME POSITIVE CHANGES
SEEDED BY THE AIDS EPIDEMIC

- The gay community coalesced in the 1980s. A strong unity emerged among gay men, whereas the community had been more fragmented in the past.
- Despite the awful manifestations of fear and homophobia, there was also an outpouring of love and support from society toward gay men.
- Many mental health clinicians generously donated their time and expertise, running support groups and offering free services to AIDS patients.
- Gay men learned that they possess greater internal strength than they would have ever realized.
- The gay community began to recognize its own power to organize, act on compassion, channel rage, and effect change.

Of course, the tragedy of AIDS is not balanced by the amount of good that emerged, but perhaps the good allows us to look back so that we can look forward with our eyes open.

THE CONTINUING IMPACT OF GRIEF

Lawrence returned to therapy because he felt that he was still living with a veil of grief from the past and that perhaps some mindfulness work would be helpful in sweeping away the residue of pain. Although he had done grief work years ago regarding the loss of his friends to AIDS, he realized that he had yet another layer to face. This is not unusual for men who lived through this difficult era. Resurgences of grief take many forms, and as newer life events take shape, there may be a need to revisit the past. I wondered out loud whether this might be the case for Lawrence and suggested we try some mindfulness exercises to explore the grief. I knew that my helping him make contact with some of the feelings related to past loss that continue to affect his inner life would allow him to find his way to a present awareness where grief has a place but doesn't seep into every place.

This client wonders how to separate from the past and still honor those he loved and lost. My perspective is simple: He has lived, and by bringing his memories forward as life lessons—rather than splitting himself between now and then—he can make the best of his gifts, which are in part enriched by all of his experience.

The success of the following script will depend in part on your own comfort. Some people might prefer to envision seats around a table or a group at the beach rather than knots along a rope. Ascertain the sensitivity of your client and choose a scenario he has referenced in the past or one that you think he may enjoy that includes a setting where a group of people can come together. The group may be people he has lost or a combination of those he has lost and those who support him now. Everyone will be included at the end of this script.

ROPE OF DESTINY

"Picture yourself in a beautiful place in nature. You can see all around you and appreciate where you are in this moment, enjoying and taking in the beautiful scenery. Appreciate the sounds, whether you are by the ocean, in the woods, or someplace else. You may hear the sound of a soft breeze rustling or of a bird chirping happily. Enjoy the scent of fresh air. That is right. Really enjoy how good it feels to be out in an open space, enjoying the vibrant place that nature provides. You and nature exist comfortably with each other. Excellent.

As you move ahead, you see a beautiful old rope draped very carefully over a railing or a chair. You are drawn to this rope, and you move closer and closer to see it and feel it.

Notice what the rope is made of, what color it is, how thin or thick it is. As you look even closer, what you see are many knots in the rope. The knots were very carefully tied. Each knot is a little different than the other. Between each knot, the amount of space is varied—some knots are closer together, while others are further apart. Appreciate how tightly or loosely the knots are tied.

I wonder if there is a way in which each knot reminds you of someone who has passed away? They may be family members, friends, or other people you have known over the course of your life who have passed on. Describe whom you see and what they look like. Notice what they are wearing and how their hair looks. How old are they in this scene? Are they quiet, or do they have something to convey to you?

You can begin to describe out loud what it is that you see as you look at each of these knots. (Alternatively, you may insert the names of the people who have passed away at each knot.) As you look at all of these knots together, you can imagine each and every one of these people supporting you simultaneously. That is right. Notice how they look at you, and listen to what they have to say to you—one person at a time or perhaps as a whole group. Appreciate what you experience inside as they support you. What it is that you are experiencing in your body at this moment, the thoughts that come up, and the emotions that emerge inside of you? That is right. Their memory and their love are things that you are able to enjoy, inside of yourself, forever."

SURVIVAL HAS A PRICE

In 1996, a new cocktail of protease inhibitors was proving successful in prolonging the lives of patients with AIDS. It offered hope. I remember this time vividly. We were hearing about the soon-to-be released protease inhibitors and were all wondering what this would mean to both clinicians and patients.

Indeed, this marked the beginning of a new landscape. We could never return to the time before people started dying, but things looked brighter. AIDS patients taking protease inhibitors had higher T-cell counts and viral loads that were undetectable or nearly undetectable.

Over the years, the cocktails have continued to improve. People are living much longer today, and the specter of HIV/AIDS is diminished. Many people who had been expecting to die went back to work and felt a sense of normalcy again. Those who had never come out to their families about being HIV positive didn't necessarily feel the need to. There was, and continues to be, a growing list of long-term survivors—a phrase that is happily used. Of course, the question arises: Why did some get to live while others did not? Many who now are doing well feel survivors' guilt.

The Rope of Destiny script imparts a message that accounts for both loss and hope in its imagery. It is a positively inclusive view for individual clients and perhaps for the community as a whole.

FURTHER TIPS FOR CONTINUING GRIEF WORK WITH CLIENTS

- Normalize, rather than minimize, when clients recognize ongoing grief.

- Encourage your client to use his own creativity and to do most of the talking.

- Suggest to your client that he will be able to integrate this grief so that it no longer takes up so much space or leeches his power. (He may feel ashamed about still feeling it after so many years.)

- Emphasize that imaginal mindfulness work will enable him to retain beautiful memories in a positive, loving way.

- Ask whom he would like to visit; remember there may be more than one person.

- Incorporate a future time projection where he views himself living happily.

- Imply optimism about your client's future.

- Invite him to ask others who have not passed away to join him if that would be beneficial.

A Mindful Moment

Exploring the multiple layers of sexuality, illness, and loss can be a lot to bear, so good preparation before you enter these explorations (and as you leave them, too) helps to establish the client's ground and reassure him that he will not lose his footing.

Help your client:

- Enjoy the ease and rhythm of each breath with his eyes closed or his gaze softened, reminding him of the life force inside of him.

- Remember that he breathes and regulates himself day in and day out without even realizing it; his body does the work that is needed.

- Acknowledge that he has faced adversity before and that despite pain, has he moved beyond it.

- Enjoy the comfort he experiences inside of himself even in this exact moment as your words reach him.

- Trust that he will continue to be able to regulate himself throughout these sessions, breathing, listening, and speaking his needs.

- Simply affirm that these mindful moments bring awareness and comfort.

UNIQUE AND COMMON EXPERIENCES

Every illness requires facing three levels of experience: 1) Coping with the illness itself, including medical treatments, protocols, diminishing health, fears about the future, etc.; 2) mourning the loss of the healthy self, including feeling unwell, vulnerable, dependent, and not able to do what once came easily; 3) sharing the experience with loved ones, who respond with their own fears and sense of loss.

What made AIDS unique was that people were dealing with their own illness while simultaneously coping with the rampant spread of the illness among friends, loved ones, and the community. Most of us begin to experience the deaths and illnesses of our peers when we are in our 60s, but AIDS took the lives of men in their 20s and 30s.

AIDS, like other extreme illness, also brought up questions about what is and what might not be an acceptable quality of life. Often, people are quite certain about what they will tolerate in terms of making quality-of-life adjustments; for example, they will never use a cane, they want to die at home, they refuse additional medication or surgery. They are sure that they want to die on their own terms without interference—but this is usually before an illness really takes hold. As people become more ill and have to make these decisions, they usually shift their perspectives, wanting to survive above all else. As therapists, we must stay attuned to these changes in attitude and be ready to work with clients at every stage of illness.

Of course, even though AIDS is more treatable now, the lingering effect of it is indelible, and sometimes gay men forget that there are other illnesses that could affect them over time. In our minds, gay men have earned "illness credit," which means that they have paid in their dues and so should be exempt from heart failure, cancer, or diabetes!

Keep in mind that clients who were diagnosed some time ago had to face the fear of death straight on. Those who are lucky enough to be alive and healthy now were at one time making preparations for death. How odd to have anticipated and planned for death and then to have been given a reprieve. As you sit with clients who have lived through their own plan for death, you can appreciate and acknowledge the impact on them whether or not they speak directly about it.

TEN WAYS TO HELP THE CLIENT WITH HIV/AIDS

1. Explore with the client lessons he learned as a result of the illness, despite the pain. Invite him to retrieve the lessons and to embrace them as guides rather than shutting them out.

2. Using scripts and exercises, introduce mindfulness as a creative way to calm the heart and open the mind to what is present, what is past, and what is possible.

3. Help the client to appreciate how the bonds of human connection, including friends, family, other support networks, and healthcare providers who care for him, are significant.

4. Encourage healthy dissociation as a way of diminishing his anxiety. Instead of going to the worst possible scenario, prompt him to suspend his fear and allow his strength to emerge and be celebrated.

5. Find where there is hope, and utilize it, amplify it.

6. Visualize a positive outcome in the present or the future. Remind him that moving from a depleted image to an expanded one will help him rebuild physical and emotional health.

7. Mention other patients as role models. Who are other people he has known who have been hopeful and strong? Encourage him to emulate their energy. Be careful not to compare; rather, let him know that these people have come through and that he can as well.

8. Imply strength and recovery: "You will get stronger." Hope will help him move forward, no matter what happens.

9. Stress the importance of positive thinking. Remind him about cognitive reframing and how it contributes to healing.

10. Use his beliefs about spirituality/philosophy to call on a language of peaceful communication (e.g., prayer, meditation, dance) with something beyond himself—god, ancestors, a universal force, the arts.

HIV/AIDS Now

The effectiveness of protease inhibitors has caused many to think of AIDS as a chronic illness that can be managed easily, with a normal life expectancy. Sometimes younger men are even willing to engage in riskier sexual behaviors because they rationalize that there are fairly simple treatment choices for HIV/AIDS that weren't available before. For older gay men, on the other hand, there is sometimes a survivor mentality that allows them to engage in risky behaviors: "I lived through it then; what do I have to lose now?" Or, "If I didn't get infected then, why would I get infected now?"

Truthfully, the risks of HIV/AIDS continue to be pronounced for gay men, and both younger and older men are getting infected with HIV (along with other sexually transmitted diseases) at high rates. Young gay men of color are being diagnosed with HIV at the highest rate. Remember that just because someone has AIDS and appears somewhat healthy, his immune system still may operate at diminished capacity. Thus, if your client gets sick, even with a simple infection, he may have a harder time fighting it off. A sinus infection can easily lead to complications that end up putting the person with a weakened immune system in the hospital. It is important to encourage a client who has AIDS to gather resources. He can live well and live long, especially if he acknowledges his vulnerability alongside his strength.

MENTAL HEALTH TREATMENT NOW

Since the landscape of HIV/AIDS has changed over the years, so have the needs of clients in therapy. Years ago, treatment helped clients prepare for illness and even death, and now the model focuses on managing the physical and emotional symptoms and using prevention techniques to maintain good health. Medical adherence and depression are key issues.

THE MOST EFFECTIVE APPROACH: A MIND-BODY APPROACH

In the late 1980s, Ann Webster of Benson-Henri Institute for Mind Body Medicine designed a 10-week mind-body program for people with HIV/AIDS in Boston. It was revolutionary at the time, one of the first such programs in the nation. The curriculum, along with Ann's enthusiasm and devotion to her clients, were part of an effective program that is still used today with great success. In fact, numerous studies show what she probably had been aware of all along—that a mindfulness meditation program, along with participation in a stress reduction group, can reduce the decline of T-cells for AIDS patients. Such groups and mindfulness practices are proven to also help with symptoms such as fever, fatigue, and pain. The benefits of participating in meditation groups include decreasing certain symptoms, but just as important is the fostering of a sense of hope and interpersonal connection. When people become ill, hope and connection are often among the first things to be lost. Given that HIV/AIDS-focused groups have become hard to find because of the overall decline in HIV/AIDS, clients should consider becoming involved in general mind-body work for support. Local hospitals and health centers often host these session.

Mind-body approaches remind people of their strengths and invite them to be in charge rather than just reacting or living strictly within the parameters of diagnosis. Being able to bring the mind-body connection into alignment makes a positive difference in how we cope with moments of great difficulty as well as the little annoyances of daily life. Participants in groups learn about stress and the warning signs; relaxation and meditation; psychoneuroimmunology studies that promote immune functioning; and homework assignments that allow them to explore on their own. Resiliency, cognitive reframing, emphasis on social support, and relapse prevention are also included. Continuing support for clients with HIV/AIDS is crucial, and combining experiential work with teaching these clients how to maintain healthy habits feeds the wellspring of successful treatment.

A MOMENT BECOMES MORE

As therapists, we see how quickly our clients strip themselves of hope in the face of illness—and, fortunately, how quickly a positive reminder takes effect so that clients can withstand the tough moments and prepare for better ones.

IN THESE CIRCUMSTANCES, MINDFULNESS STRATEGIES ARE INTEGRAL TO:

- Relaxation
- Boosting mental and physical health
- Decreasing anxiety
- Increasing a sense of hope
- Allowing space to distinguish between past and present symptoms
- Reclaiming positive coping mechanisms and self-confidence
- Letting time be slow when there is a feeling of pleasure and allowing it to pass when there is pain

---

Many people are afraid that unless they have a formal practice of mindfulness, and unless their practice consists of at least 20 minutes once or twice a day, they are not doing enough. I stress the significance of a "mindful moment" or a "minute of mindfulness." I suggest that the benefits of pausing to recollect are numerous. It helps us center, returning to a comfortable place inside, and to enhance positive coping, as we align with healthier, less distorted thinking. You can ask your client to close his eyes for a few moments and then help him center himself in his body by appreciating the flow of each in-breath and out-breath, noticing the sounds in the room, or visualizing a place of contentment, a scene in nature or a vacation spot that is meaningful. These sorts of practices are basic and easily facilitated and serve as a reminder to clients that they have the ability to modulate their own states.

The following is a basic script that can be adapted to suit the context and the client's style. Remember to use the strength of your own voice to emphasize optimism. You can adapt my words to your needs depending on the situation or symptoms your client is experiencing. No matter what, you will be implying that he has the ability to feel better in the future. Instilling hope is important; it alleviates stress—and stress only exacerbates symptoms and depression.

ENHANCING COMFORT

"You can appreciate the way in which your body is sitting comfortably in this moment. Take your time to breathe deeply and relax. Enjoy the ways in which it feels comfortable to sit here right now, to appreciate how it feels as you take the space and create the time to be quiet and mindful. That is right.

You can enjoy these sensations of relaxation. There may be moments when you forgot to be attentive to this part of yourself, to your mind, your body, and your emotional self. You can benefit from this moment and moments like this in the future. Excellent. Stillness, quietness, and relaxation really provide a great benefit. You are reminded, once again, how attainable this is. You feel good, and you will remember this moment.

You know that there are many ups and downs throughout various days of your life, like the bouncing of a ball, up and down, down and up, and up and down again. Even though you would wish you felt perfect day in and day out, life isn't like that. It really makes sense in this moment. You can endure these ups and these downs with greater strength, and you know how strong you can be, since you have been strong many times in the past. You might even remember a time when you felt uncertain about your own sense of strength, and yet, you were able to get beyond a struggle because of your own natural strengths.

As you remember this time, allow yourself in this moment to enjoy the physical sensations you feel inside. Remember that you can have passing moments of comfort inside, and they can last for longer periods each time you practice this because of your own existing strength.

Inside of you, in the back of your mind, are all kinds of memories and experiences that remind you that you have had the ability to cope and to be strong—to be strong and to grow. Inside of you, you know you have done this many times already in your life.

This might even include being gay—taking the risk to acknowledge this to yourself and then to others. Yes, it was difficult doing what was best for you while feeling a sense of uncertainty about what the outcome might be, but as you are here in this moment, you appreciate that things worked out just right for you. That is right.

You can continue to see this and know this for yourself now as well. I wonder if you can envision your future by seeing your healthier self emerging in your own mind right now. You don't have to strive for perfection; you know that comfort or feeling good enough will do just fine for you. You can see yourself in the future, feeling comfortable, feeling strong, being confident in your own abilities to get through each day, each week, each month, with certainty, strength, and good enough health. That is right.

Just as you knew long ago about the ups and downs of life and how you could use your strength back then, you can use your strength right now to keep yourself moving forward, to enjoy the momentum of time as it unfolds, to appreciate the growing sense of strength inside of you that continues and continues and continues along, so you can flourish. Excellent!"

To incorporate if your client is feverish:

"You can remember dipping into a nice clear lake filled with fresh water on a summer day when you felt so hot that you wanted to cool yourself down. How refreshing that clear water was to your body as you went into the water. How enjoyable it felt to be able to bring yourself to coolness. How immediately and in this moment, too, everything can feel better."

To incorporate if your client has chills:

"You can also appreciate the feeling of sitting by a fire in the wintertime. The sounds of the wood crackling or the orange embers throwing off heat from the flames of the fire, providing warmth, not only to your body, but to your emotional self, too."

PREVENTION
HELPING HIV-NEGATIVE CLIENTS REMAIN NEGATIVE

Times are changing, and this is good. Truvada, a combination medication originally used for HIV infection within 28 days of exposure to the virus, has a newer application as well: It is now being used to keep HIV-negative people from becoming infected, and the results are astonishing. It is suggested by the drug company that taking this medication daily, along with employing safer sexual practices, will greatly decrease the likelihood of getting infected with HIV. It is reported that it is 92 to 99 percent effective in preventing the transmission of HIV. For those who prefer to only take it four times a week instead of seven, the prevention of transmission is still in the low 90th percentile. There is a great deal of literature available online, but the best sources are LGBT health centers, the Centers for Disease Control (CDC), and AIDS service organizations.

Pre-Exposure Prophylaxis (PrEP) was approved in 2012. Many saw this as "the miracle drug." It caught on slowly in larger cities in the United States, including New York City and San Francisco, yet there was a lot of controversy and confusion surrounding it. A daily regimen of this medication has proven to reduce the risk of HIV by 99 percent for men having sex with men (MSM). What were/are the issues?

First, many healthcare providers were not aware of its use for this purpose. Perhaps the drug companies hadn't marketed it sufficiently, assuming that it was so effective that once it was approved by the FDA, medical providers would simply promote its use, making marketing seem unnecessary. Also, unless insurance companies reimbursed for the cost, many people could not afford to take the daily dose. Still, why were so many doctors not advocating for the use of PrEP? Did they not trust it would work? Were they fearful that more men would have intercourse without condoms? Or was something else preventing their recommending PrEP?

Think about it: How long it has taken gay men and medical personnel to find a comfort zone regarding gay sexuality and the diminishment of risk? Suddenly, there is an incredible opportunity, but we, as care providers, are scared. Healthcare providers were vicariously traumatized by the AIDS epidemic, too. Perhaps PrEP triggers the fears that surround sexuality, illness, and death. Perhaps old traumas were and are resurfacing regarding HIV/AIDS and more liberal sexual practices. The Pandora's box that was sealed opened all over again. Who is to say that medical providers should trust the drug companies anyway? Many people do not trust them. I suspect that these are some of the reasons why PrEP didn't catch on as quickly as anticipated. Furthermore, subtle forms of homophobia are always part of the puzzle.

Five Questions to Ask Yourself Before Talking to Clients About PrEP

DIRECTIONS: Once you understand the uses and potential of PrEP, answer the following questions to assess your comfort in working with your clients as they consider it as a part their sexual lives.

- How does the introduction of PrEP frighten you (whether or not the reasoning is logical)?

- Does the topic elicit subtle forms of homophobia in you?

- What is your reaction to the fact that the use of PrEP indirectly encourages a free expression of sexuality?

- Even though you know that taking PrEP reduces transmission of HIV, how do you feel about your client having sex without condoms?

- If your client takes PrEP but not regularly, how will you intervene with him?

Now, let's think about these issues from a client's point of view. Unless he lives in a large city, how will he learn about this medication? He may feel ashamed to ask his medical doctor for it or may even find that he has to tell his doctor about it.

Gay men are becoming more accepting of PrEP, and its use is catching on. It is now estimated that 15 to 20 percent of at-risk men are using it, and this number is increasing quickly. PrEP is now in the public eye more; doctors, nurses, therapists, and HIV workers are promoting it. As one 30-year-old sexually active client said, "As long as I am single and being sexually free, it is my responsibility to take PrEP for the safety of myself and others." Later that week, a 60-year-old client said, "I just can't believe how lucky we are to be able to have access to this medication. I lost a lover to HIV, and now I can have sex with less worry. I never imagined a day like this."

Certain hookup apps actually have a category for those who identify themselves as being on PrEP, another way to raise awareness about what PrEP is and how to use it. With apps that don't have a category for use of PrEP, men are openly promoting their use of it on their profiles. Sexual health is on the rise.

Regularly adhering to the PrEP dosage and schedule may indirectly foster greater mindfulness, in that it keeps health in the forefront, which may decrease impulsiveness. As a therapist, you have already learned something about PrEP, and perhaps you will read up on it in greater depth, so that your gay clients will feel supported and understood by you in this part of their life, too.

Therapists working with gay men who may benefit from PrEP can encourage their clients to do their homework, speak to a doctor, get information and feedback from peers, find out about insurance coverage, look for clinical trials if insurance won't cover it, celebrate the decision to take it, envision setting up the schedule and adhering to it, and work out in advance how they will tell others that they are taking it.

NEWLY DIAGNOSED CLIENTS

Given that not everybody is taking PrEP, there are still moments where exposure to HIV puts someone at risk. Using drugs and/or alcohol can diminish judgment, and frequently exposure to HIV occurs in these circumstances. It is strongly suggested that if a gay man has put himself at risk of HIV he contact a physician or go to an emergency room to go on PEP (Post-Exposure Prophylaxis) within 72 hours. PEP is a cocktail of three antiretroviral HIV medications to reduce the risk of becoming HIV positive. It is administered for 28 days.

A good psychotherapy relationship includes ongoing honest discussions regarding sexuality. Therefore, if your client has put himself at risk, ideally, he will bring this up to you and you will strongly encourage him to contact a doctor and go on PEP. You will also want to explore the situation that led to his decision, help him to evaluate the nuances of his decision, and in subsequent sessions, anticipate how he can shift his behavior in the future. I have worked with clients who haven't confessed their behaviors to me within the 72-hour window. Even so, the sooner they seek medical help, the better off they are.

Being diagnosed as HIV positive today may not be the death sentence it was several years ago. HIV is a virus that is considered to be manageable and may not shorten someone's life span, but it is still an emotionally painful experience. A lot of important decisions need to be made, including where to find the best medical care. Finding a clinic or hospital that has current treatment protocols is essential. In addition, for men who haven't come out to their physicians, it is essential to come out, reveal their HIV status, or switch providers to be able to address the significant issues unique to HIV. I have worked with some men who have kept their long-term family physician without disclosing that they are gay and have worked with others who ignored their HIV status for years because it brought up too much shame or fear.

Undoubtedly, there is great deal of stigma and judgment toward men who seroconvert in this day and age. "Shouldn't they know better?" is a common question that medical personnel and therapists ask each other. I can't help but wonder how transparent our thoughts are as clients, who already are experiencing so much pain, search our faces for solace. Of course, factors such as attachment needs and the use of substances influence decisions made in the heat of the moment regarding unsafe sex.

As mentioned earlier, cases of HIV/AIDS are multiplying most rapidly among gay men of color under the age of 30. Any therapist treating gay men—especially young gay men of color, should have information brochures and newsletters on safe sex and HIV/AIDS readily available in their office. (Contact the CDC or AIDS organizations for literature.) The CDC is expanding their outreach efforts toward HIV prevention among young men of color. They are finding a decrease in sexual health, low rates of HIV testing, decreased condom use, and higher rates of STDs in this population. Because young people aren't as concerned about infection, greater efforts are being made to educate them. Consider discussing this casually and comfortably with your younger gay clients so they can educate themselves about safety.

Reassure your clients that when they are first diagnosed, it may feel like life will never return to normal, but it will—to a new normal. I cite examples of people with whom I have worked, sharing how they struggled in the beginning, never imagining that their day-to-day life would be okay again, but that it has gotten better and easier over time. I reassure each client that this will be the case for him as well. Even when it seems as though a client is doing well, I let him hear these supportive words.

In addition to clarifying the array of current treatment options available compared with what clients remember or have been told about what was available in decades past, I also encourage them to establish a support network to check in with—ideally people who understand HIV/AIDS or even have it and serve as healthy role models. Suggesting a pychoeducational group for newly diagnosed people is also ideal if such groups are offered in your area.

It is important to live responsibly, getting good medical care, engaging in healthy sex, and taking care of oneself to live a balanced life. What's more, living life as a whole person, rather than just an HIV patient is a healthy way to live. Often, we are taught that compartmentalization is not a good way to live and is counter to being responsible and balanced; however, there is healthy compartmentalization, which many of us actually encourage in doing experiential work. *Healthy denial* is a term I like sharing with my clients. Being prepared for what may come along further down the road is a good thing, but living life as a healthy, strong male who can put aside thoughts of illness and death plays an important role in prevention and in coping with being newly diagnosed with HIV.

WHAT TO ADDRESS WITH
NEWLY DIAGNOSED CLIENTS

Following are the eight central areas of concern that need to be considered as you sit with a client who has been newly diagnosed as HIV positive.

1. **DISCLOSING HIV STATUS**: Since people aren't necessarily becoming ill following diagnosis, it is reasonable for your clients to decide not to tell family members or friends if they don't feel ready or deem it necessary. I suggest that they do have a couple of people (such as friends or peers) in whom to confide.

   Having plenty of time to prioritize readiness for self-disclosure and follow-up with you is important during this time.

2. **MEDICAL CONCERNS FOLLOWING DIAGNOSIS**: Your client won't be able to predict how the quality of his life will be. Often, the first onset of a cold or flu is scary. It may take a few rounds of normal illness to accept that every symptom isn't necessarily connected to HIV.

   Getting blood work done may also stir up anxiety, and blood is drawn every 3 to 6 months. Most people develop a greater sense of comfort after going through this cycle a few times.

3. **WHEN TO BEGIN TAKING HIV AND PSYCHOTROPIC MEDICATIONS**: This is an important decision that is made by your client and his doctor. Considerations include current treatment protocols; adherence to taking medications, which can be complicated; the psychological reactions of starting these new medications, which make normal denial impossible; and managing the side effects of the medications.

   Drugs used to treat HIV/AIDS can cause psychological reactions, such as depression, anxiety, and other issues. Thus, psychotropic medications to regulate these conditions may be advisable. Educating your client about the significance of managing these symptoms is crucial for medical adherence and overall good health. Your job is to help your client assess what will be most useful to him. He may engage in mindfulness techniques, take medication, or opt for a combination of mindfulness and medication.

4. **SEXUALITY**: How does your client navigate sex now that he knows his status? Among the issues: how to routinely practice safer sex, incorporating the awareness that there are still risks to having unsafe sex even in a monogamous relationship, and discerning whether it is necessary to disclose HIV status to random sexual partners.

Remember, your job is not to police whether he discloses his status; far more important is for you to encourage safer sex guidelines whether or not his status is disclosed. A good way for your client to think about this is to imagine that every new sexual partner is HIV positive. This approach encourages safer sex practices while bypassing the necessity of having to ask questions or disclose. Often, gay men who discuss their HIV status with a new sexual partner end up having a prematurely intimate conversation, which can be difficult on either side of this discussion.

Contrary to what some of your clients may believe, they cannot tell if someone is HIV positive. There are many healthy asymptomatic men with HIV.

Of course, not every person is honest about his status. Some men actually lie. This can be more common on sexual hook-up sites, where a potential partner may be overly eager for a sexual connection or is high on substances. Men who are overly eager for attachment (as opposed to sexuality) may do anything to get these needs met.

5. **LIFESTYLE**: Proper sleep hygiene and good diet are important for a healthy immune system. Again, relaxation and mindfulness can enhance immune functioning. Work with your clients to emphasize these correlations and teach them techniques that they can easily use outside your office.

Other options include alternative medical practices such as acupuncture or massage. It is very satisfying to discover new resources with your client.

6. **LEGAL ARRANGEMENTS**: Encourage your client to make proper legal arrangements, such as medical proxy, power of attorney, and updating or creating a will.

7. **DEPRESSION**: Depression is prevalent among people who are HIV positive, whether it is due to the psychosocial stressors inherent with HIV/AIDS or side effects of medications. Working to minimize or prevent depression is essential. Depression gets in the way of your client enjoying the life he has and can affect the level of self-care he pursues. Scientific studies reveal a faster viral load increase and rapid decline in T cells in patients who are depressed. Depression is also correlated with higher levels of substance abuse and riskier sexual behavior.

Therapy has two distinct streams with clients who are newly diagnosed: to enhance a sense of purpose and meaning in life and to encourage adherence to medical support. These kinds of interventions will greatly impact your client. Remember the significance of the therapeutic relationship. Your interactions can enhance his optimism.

8. **SUPPORTS AND PEER INPUT**: The significance of having ongoing support from friends or peers is apparent. Consider a referral to a support or therapy group if needed. Look for a mind-body group or an experiential therapy group that teaches skills in mindfulness and relaxation.

Also encourage meaningful social and familial relationships as a way to maintain optimism and good health. Sometimes, completely new interests may be discovered in the effort to widen the client's social network, such as clubs, charities, competitions, and other activities.

Activities in which clients offer guidance and support to others can also enhance quality of life. Meaning can be derived from the experience of having HIV/AIDS when the person is able to share what he knows and offer the kind of support that only someone with the diagnosis can provide.

Tools and Resources

As we said, despite advancements in medical care, receiving a diagnosis of HIV is still traumatic, and it takes some time to figure out how to best navigate the medical and mental health system. As a therapist, you have much to offer in the way of tools and other resources.

If you live in a large city, there may be agencies that offer LGBT services or, more specifically, medical or social service agencies that offer assistance to people with HIV/AIDS. Many of these provide psychoeducational material and useful information, including cutting-edge treatment protocols.

When I have a newly diagnosed client, I pair him up with someone else diagnosed with HIV/AIDS who can speak to him about the trials and tribulations ahead. This has proven to be very valuable: At times, I think that clients get more from peers than they do from me. What is key in making such a referral is finding somebody who is pragmatic, reassuring, and positive and has useful insights and can offer support.

Discordant Couples

When one partner is HIV negative and the other positive, there are many things at stake. First and foremost is how the couple will navigate sexually. What behaviors will they engage in, and what do they want to risk? Depending on sexual preferences, will the negative partner take PrEP? The myriad issues the couple will face also include self-disclosure for each partner, since individual needs for support may differ, and the painful conversations must take place, including what should happen if the HIV-infected partner becomes ill or dies.

When you meet with these couples or work with one partner individually, you want to provide an honest and safe forum that encourages the exploration of all of these details. Couples therapy is fruitful when honesty, compassion, and nonjudgmental interaction are in place. Fortunately, with currently available treatments, these conversations are can revolve more around good planning than impending suffering.

Simply Put

Therapists who work with gay men—or even one gay man—need to know that HIV/AIDS is part of the backdrop of the entire gay community. No matter a client's age or personal history, he has been touched by it even if he is not conscious of how. The effects seem to be nearly impossible to integrate. Thus, therapists need to be aware of the history and current course of HIV, the consequences of infection, preventative approaches, obstacles to safe practice, the resources available, and so much more.

The first step, however, is self-assessment. We may assume that all therapists are or should be comfortable dealing with illness or death, but this simply is not true. Personal experience and age are just two of the factors that may affect your comfort level. The good news is that experiential work is especially powerful in helping clients to integrate past losses and evolving lessons. The comfort that you will observe developing in your clients will affect you as well.

6 | Religion, Spirituality, and Integration

How times have changed in the spheres of religion and spirituality. Various religious denominations are not only welcoming gay congregants but also gay clergy. There are now gay rabbis and ministers. Just a generation ago, gays were totally shut out, but now there are many places for those who are religious to worship and feel embraced.

Along similar lines is the increased global recognition and acceptance of gay marriage equality. This has profound political and religious implications. Spouses are now eligible to receive a husband's federal benefits; they are acknowledged in hospitals as health care proxies; and they can inherit when there is no will rather than everything automatically going to the next of kin.

A gay couple can now marry in a church or synagogue. Think about it. Previous to gay marriage, gay men and society in general consciously and unconsciously promoted an inferior status of gays and lesbians by not allowing them the same rights as others. All of this is changing, and rather quickly. This will continue to have positive ramifications for gay men: self-acceptance and societal acceptance. Over the next several years, we will watch the parameters continue to expand, including a greater level of flexibility from religious institutions.

Although we can rejoice in this, we cannot simply turn away from all that has happened in the past. Gay men have endured pain that is lasting; for many adults the damage has already been done. Being reared in communities that endorse the intolerant doctrines of many religious institutions has left scars for many gay men who continue to feel disenfranchised and isolated. Often, their families of origin and the communities in which they were raised still don't accept them. Unfortunately, being gay is still viewed as a sin according to most conservative religious groups.

The suffering of having grown up being ridiculed, chastised, and taught that one's sexual orientation is evil simply doesn't go away later in life. The message remains imbedded in the soul. Despite the current more liberal climate, there are plenty of conservative institutions and prominent leaders that still do not condone homosexuality. Being gay is still considered immoral by some. Going to hell in the afterlife is the fate that many people hold in store for gays. Many of my clients, despite being out for years and comfortable with who they are, still grapple with the old messages that continue to haunt them.

There is a wide spectrum of current religious institutions, from those that are open to LBGT members to those that are not at all open. Conservative religious groups express hostility towards gays and engage in censorship, distortion, and blatant discrimination. How do family members who hold these beliefs not hurt our gay clients? How do gay men raised in these environments come away unscathed? They don't.

Even now, conversion therapy, which is aimed at "converting" people from gay to heterosexual, is promoted among some people. Despite the fact that it has been deemed unethical by most U.S. medical and mental health organizations, some groups (frequently of the Christian right) continue to send their sons and daughters to conversion therapy to "fix their illness." This practice often leads to depression, suicidal ideation, or actual suicide attempts. Yes, this option still exists.

There is good news, too. As our society continues to modernize, conservative organizations are losing members. This is a sign of changing times. Friends and families of gays are voicing their concerns and finding the strength to walk away in support of their loved ones. Some conservative groups are starting to loosen their strict regulations as a matter of survival.

It would not be a surprise if you, as a therapist, were impatient with a client who is negatively affected by his religious/spiritual background but refuses to leave it behind. You want him to feel more at ease, more accepting of himself. It seems obvious to you: The way to not struggle is to leave that belief system. The answer is never this simple, though, since what has been embedded comes from a complicated history rather than a pragmatic choice in the present. If the client could make choices so easily and live them so freely, he would. So, now it is your turn: Consider how you can practice your own mindfulness to reach a wider understanding, a more accepting stance. Sometimes we are the ones who benefit the most from the mindful awareness we proffer.

BELIEFS BEHIND BELIEFS

DIRECTIONS: Take a moment to consider your own religious or spiritual beliefs and how they might come up in your work with your client. Answer simply and honestly, selecting options from the 3-point scale, with "1" representing "not at all," "2," "somewhat," and "3," "very much."

- Are you a religious person?   1   2   3

- Do you see yourself as spiritual?   1   2   3

- Are you bothered when a client actively expresses religious/spiritual beliefs different from your own?   1   2   3

- Are you bothered when a client has more pronounced religious/spiritual views than your own?   1   2   3

- Are you bothered when a client holds no religious/spiritual beliefs?
                                                                                                          1   2   3

- Is it difficult to tolerate it when a client's religious/spiritual upbringing has caused him to hate himself?   1   2   3

- Would you be willing to work with a parent or family member whose religious/spiritual beliefs limit any ability to emotionally support a gay relative?

  _____

  _____

- Do your religious or spiritual beliefs influence how you view your client's understanding of his own dilemmas or areas of emotional confusion?

  _____

  _____

DOES GOD HATE GAY PEOPLE?

Your client comes into treatment. Religious belief is not his stated issue, yet it may be at the root of many issues in his daily life. Unresolved issues related to religion may actually be lurking beneath emotional struggles with family, anxiety, depression, substance abuse, or sexual addiction. Because being gay is considered to be a sin in some religions, those who have internalized this message still carry an internal fragmentation. Society in general tends to reinforce a less-than view of gay people. This felt sense of splintered identity has an insidious impact on a variety of behaviors. Additionally, religion is usually just one of multiple contexts, such as family, community, school, media, in which fear, bias, and ignorance intersect. Gay boys who grew up in conservative religious families certainly may have experienced more trauma and psychological difficulties than others. The profound discontinuity between a client's identity and that of his family and church may still plague him, even years after coming out. In fact, he may be more conservative than other gay men. In other words, he may be less accepting—even of himself. Feelings of constant shame may unconsciously persist into his adulthood. Living life in partial secrecy is a common response. His self-expression, wardrobe choices, or even whom he chooses as friends and partners may be limited by it.

Because compartmentalization is common, internalized homophobia manifests in more deceptive ways, including alcohol abuse or other substance abuse, excessive masturbation, and sexual compulsivity, all which may mask deeper issues. Self-loathing is at the core, and the splitting off that is instrumental to the client's survival may result in a higher incidence of unsafe sexual behaviors and other destructive tendencies.

Unfortunately, some parents, particularly fathers, follow the doctrine of certain religious teachings rather than take the lead in the acceptance of their own gay sons. The damage that is caused is never forgotten.

THE CLIENT'S ONGOING JOURNEY

Many clients who are conservative in their religious beliefs feel trapped: Who they are and who they are supposed to be are at odds. It is the impasse that is common to gay men's general life experience, fraught with conflict. With religion, this dilemma arises in relation the very place that is supposed to offer comfort to all. Many people have no idea how to even begin to work on reconciling this deeply personal struggle. However, a gay man's life can truly shift through finding a religious institution that can help him to accept himself, along with support from a mental health professional to bring the questions and solutions out into the open.

Once it is established that a client is having difficulty reconciling how religion or spirituality was seen in his family of origin and how he lives his life, the therapist can encourage him to think about a series of issues that may be having an ongoing powerful impact. The following questions are meant to bring out the context of his current struggle and perhaps point therapist and client in the direction of solutions. Even just the task of filling out the assessment can lessen the intensity of conflict, because being able to delineate and elaborate feelings can help move tension out of the body and help a client get into a more neutral emotional space.

A Mindful Moment

Reminding the client to center himself and build self-awareness will go a long way in helping him to maintain his rootedness in the present as he teach you about his past. Keep in mind that religion often creates the most intense feelings of guilt and shame.

Take some time to invite your client to:

- Go into the deep comfortable space where he has been with you before, breathing in fresh clean air and breathing out any tension or stress

- Acknowledge that he is able to choose to enjoy this moment, and that this feeling of serenity will continue to be available to him

- Appreciate the awareness of the safety and strength of his body, which affirms a certainty of self and separateness from others

- Remember that he has taken care of himself in a variety of positive ways over the course of his lifetime

- Know that he already possesses everything he needs to continue making sacred connections

- Feel himself as an adult—currently safe and free

BELIEFS BEHIND BELIEFS:
AN ASSESSMENT TO USE WITH YOUR CLIENTS

Use the following assessment with your client to find out their beliefs behind beliefs. Have your client answer the following questions as honestly as possible. Then, use the space below to invite him to identify strategies to reconcile conflicts regarding religion or spirituality and current beliefs.

You will need to tease out your client's feelings about religion and spirituality in order to discern his current needs. Based on how he answers the questions, you can ascertain whether possible solutions might be more external or internal in nature—it is likely some combination. The following ideas are some examples that may prime your imagination as you look to supporting your clients.

=CLIENT ASSESSMENT=
BELIEFS BEHIND BELIEFS

DIRECTIONS: Please answer the following questions as honestly as possible.

- How religious was your family and the community in which you grew up? (Assuming that religion was a part of the client's upbringing, continue with the following questions.)

_____

- How did growing up in your religious family shape your experience of coming out?

_____

- How did growing up in your religious family shape your experience of what it meant to gay?

_____

- Can you identify the lingering effects as an adult?

_____

- How was homosexuality viewed in your church, synagogue, or mosque (or other place of worship)?

_____

- Have you avoided coming out to your family because of their religious beliefs?

_____

- Did your family believe in an anti-gay doctrine?

_____

- Has your religion used words such as *evil*, *sin*, or *abomination* to define or refer to homosexuality?

  _____

- Do these ideas infiltrate your notions of what is and what is not okay with regard to your sexuality?

  _____

- Do you believe that there is as an afterlife? If the answer is yes, what does being gay mean in terms of the afterlife?

  _____

- Have you ever felt as though you have needed to choose between being gay and being religious? If so, how have you reconciled the "choices?" Has this shifted over time?

  _____

- If you have current religious or spiritual beliefs, have you found an accepting community?

  _____

- If you do not believe now but grew up with religion, how have you been able to separate from your family and/or congregation's ideas? Is the separation peaceful or fraught with difficulty?

  _____

- If you don't hold formal religious beliefs, do you imagine there is something or someone other than a godlike figure looking after you from "above" or "beyond?" Explain.

  _____

- If your current understanding is purely secular, are you comfortable with it?

  _____

What Resolution Might Look Like For Various Clients

By now you, have explored a variety of internal and external resources with your client. It is time to invite him to expand on the ideas by coming up with some strategies to implement one or more of them.

Together, you and your client will consider the following spheres of internal resolution:

- Ways to further self-acceptance regardless of social standards
- Identify the independent choices he has made in other areas in his life and seeing how they can be applied personally
- Explore more expansive dimensions of faith or prayer that can offer comfort
- Use mindfulness as a means to settle into greater self-acceptance and comfort
- Find role models who are inspiring

Together you will identify viable external solutions:

- Locate supportive places of worship for gays and lesbians
- Discover new spiritual or philosophical paths that provide what will be helpful now
- Create a new community that may or may not be bonded by a specific religious/spiritual belief
- Update the client's information about how the religious landscape is changing with regard to gays and lesbians (moving beyond old understandings)
- Speak with gay clergy for validation and support

Parents, Religion, and Gay Men

Gay men who struggle with religion and identity often have experienced a combination of fear and conflict growing up, especially with their fathers. A father who is religious may not be able to see beyond his religious understanding or to appreciate contemporary themes regarding being gay. The gay child or adult hits a wall with his father that feels impenetrable. The father may not have the will to question or challenge his belief structures and thus must reject his gay son in order to stay in accord with his beliefs. He rejects his son because the son is gay and being gay is against his religion. The rejection is felt by the son on both levels—first as a renunciation of homosexuality and second, on a deeper level, as a repudiation of himself. A father's disapproval can erode a son's sense of masculinity and respect, even into adulthood. The son in turn feels neither masculine enough nor acceptable to God.

A mother's religious belief system may be equally challenging, but often the mother–gay son bond is strong enough to overcome conflicting beliefs. Frequently, the mother is the primary caretaker who allows her connection to her gay son to flourish no matter what. To be clear, I am not saying that all mothers are supportive. Her loyalty to the church may outweigh her connection with her son. But in my experience, the tension between mothers and sons tends to be less than that with fathers.

The challenge for families is huge because when a son comes out to his parents and they are part of a conservative religious sect, the parents have to find a way to cope with a heart-rending division: losing connection with a child or feel shamed and perhaps outcast in the religious community. Oddly enough, if parents could compartmentalize, life might be easier. They could separate out the teaching of the religion from the love for their child and then choose to have a connection with their child.

"You are my son, and I love you no matter what" is the ideal sentiment that a parent can convey to a child, regardless of age, and it does happen. An adult gay man who has avoided coming out to his parents and finds the courage to do so as an adult still craves validation from his parents: "You are our son."

For parents who are conflicted about having a gay son but open to finding support, connecting with PFLAG (Parents and Friends of Lesbians and Gays), a peer-run group can be both educational and supportive.

WHEN IMPLICATION TRUMPS CONFRONTATION

Sometimes, unspoken moments of acceptance are as powerful as spoken ones, and we need to help our clients tease these moments out and receive them. Mike, for example, is a client whose parents don't approve of his lifestyle but nevertheless visited him in the gay resort where he lives. They occasionally ask how is partner is doing, implicitly acknowledging his presence and importance. Mike may wish for more, but I remind him that in their way, his parents are demonstrating acceptance of his being gay.

Mike continues to feel self-conscious about being gay with his family despite years of being out. He recently married his partner in a private ceremony. He resisted sharing the news with his conservative family and didn't post it on Facebook for this reason. On a visit home for the holidays, he was in a quandary about whether he would wear his wedding band. With coaching from me and a support group, he decided to keep the ring on and prepared himself to answer any questions that might come up. (He decided to focus on the legal benefits available to him as a spouse in his explanation, especially because he and his partner have been together for many years.) He wore a few rings on both hands with the hope of distracting his family! Nobody asked about the wedding band, and he was relieved. The consensus among the group was that on some level, his family was aware of the ring on his left finger but chose to keep things civil, just as Mike had wanted.

Less than ideal are families who might "accept" remaining close to their gay son but not accepting his partner. Even if they don't reject their child, they may reject their child's lifestyle, partner, and friends, all of which, of course, is experienced as rejection. In these instances, the gay man has to choose between tolerating the partial acceptance from his family or setting limits and not agreeing to his family's parameters, which may result in silence or estrangement.

One strategy is to encourage your client to indirectly reinforce his lifestyle with his parents without being confrontative, as I did with Jay. His parents know full well that he is gay and lives with his partner, and they told him that they do not feel comfortable visiting him in Boston because of this relationship and living arrangement. Jay continues to visit his family in their home town and with my encouragement has decided to occasionally make simple, casual references to "we" (referring to him and his partner) or to speak about him and Dave with his nieces and nephews. The implication is that he is in a partnership with a man, and his nieces and nephews know about it whether or not it is mentioned. He has even chosen to do this in his parents' presence, with the awareness that they won't challenge him in front of the kids. In the presence of his siblings (the kids' parents), who are accepting, he experiences a greater sense of camaraderie.

ACCEPTING WHAT IS: FINDING A NEW COMMUNITY

With the rise in the number of states legalizing gay marriage, the dialogue in families and in society in general has opened up to an extent. Even in certain conservative circles, there is some attention being given to the conversation. With a wider array of options available for worship and contemplation, many more men are able to meet their spiritual needs in gathering places that are affirming. Community and acceptance are healing and powerful. Many churches now welcome their gay congregants, and there are gay networks and support groups within many congregations. For some men, this support can be more significant than psychotherapy because having affirmation from a minister or congregation can heal earlier experiences and provide that layer of spiritual life that they crave.

Unfortunately, many gay men who grew up in more conservative religions have internalized beliefs that are so shaming that switching churches doesn't undo the damage. No matter what, they view themselves as sinners. This internalization is so deep that there is little that we as therapists can do to convince them that they are okay. This is a painful reality. Assuming that social consciousness continues to evolve, however, we can look forward to greater acceptance both from others and within ourselves. As therapists, we are at the forefront of this shift.

= CASE EXCERPT =

SEAN

Sean is a 51-year-old gay client who grew up in a conservative Mormon family. He was always religious and felt great conflict about being gay: "*In my religion, homosexuality is compared to murder, and those who participate in it are treated as such in the afterlife. My sexuality started oozing out of me. I told my bishop I was feeling an overwhelming sense of passion toward men, and he told me the church doesn't accept that. These were dark emotional times because I felt I was doing wrong, yet at the same time felt I was doing what I needed to do.*"

To free himself, Sean decided to move to the Northeast in the hope of leading a more progressive life. However, being torn between his religious roots and an urban gay lifestyle was a constant struggle. He never found ease in his choices and often feared that the Holy Ghost was watching him: "*I got tired of lying to my parents and finally told them I was gay. Both of them told me I was condemned. My father told me that gay marriage is a sin, and that if I was disillusioned with the church, it was because the church does not support sin. I was heartbroken.*"

Sean decided that the only way he could totally free himself was to excommunicate himself from the church. He told his family, and though they were sad, they remained loyal and wanted to maintain a loving connection. Years later, his conflict about religion resurfaced. While visiting his parents, his father casually asked him if he would consider re-joining the church. "*I remember the Biblical term 'building a house on sand' and feared that everything that I had in my life was going to get washed away,*" he said. During this bleak period, Sean was afraid that indeed he was a sinner and that the gay life he created for himself would erode and he would end up being punished in his next life.

Sean agreed to three interventions

- Join a gay male therapy group

- See a psychopharmacologist

- Utilize experiential work with me to explore the use of his own strength to comfort himself

Fortunately, all three were good resources. The group gave him the opportunity to voice his fears with other gay men, some of whom had grown up in religious families and had needed to reconcile their own ambivalence. The support and shared experience helped him not feel so alone. The compassionate care from his doctor and the medication that Sean agreed to take helped him manage anxiety and depression. That, in turn, gave him the respite he needed to build up his strength. In our experiential collaboration, we did ego-strengthening work with the goal of allowing Sean to feel more grounded and steady.

Three excerpts from our very powerful hypnosis sessions follow. I begin each session with a basic induction and invite Sean to use his own creativity to explore thoughts, feelings, and visual images that prevent him from reconciling being gay with his religious background.

Session One

Sean: "*I'm coming off some upper deck stairs outside onto a patio. There is a nice swinging sofa made of wood with soft cushions. The temperature is dry, and the sun feels good on my skin. I see my cat coming up to me. I feel vulnerable, as if something bad will happen, but from now on in my life, I am allowing good moments to be good moments.*"

This image emphasizes Sean's ability to use resources and to feel vulnerability and pleasure simultaneously. Also, having his cat nearby reflects the positive imagery with animals that is often powerful in experiential work.

Session Two

Sean: "*I see gingham plaid on the tops of jars, which are evocative of Midwest family values. They are red, aqua, black, and brown in simple styles. The front of the jars have drawings of faces on them. There is a devil's head, a bunny's head, and a kitty's head.*"

The interpretation of experiential work is always unique to each individual. It is interesting how Sean incorporates both his current life and his struggles in this scene. His family's values are important and pleasant, which he is able to see and describe. At the same time, the heads on the jars are metaphors for what he experiences in his life, the interplay between playful childlike nurturing animals and the devil. Seeing these jars side by side, another metaphor, Sean experienced a sense of relief for being able to simultaneously contain all his struggles and still feel whole.

SESSION THREE

Sean is returning home to see his parents. This is the first visit since the conversation with his father about joining the church again that had sent him into a tailspin. He is filled with uncertainty about what may happen: "*I am swimming in a sea of shame. I fear more tears after that last trip. I feel a pressure in my chest, that Holy Ghost feeling. I don't want a scary religious moment where the church is more important than everything else.*"

Then something shifts within him; it happens quickly and automatically: "*I can go on with my day. The message from God feels like a burning in the bosom, but I really do understand that my father's question about going back to the church was just that. It really wasn't about me but about what he was taught regarding religion in his own life. I feel less resentful toward him.*" The shift is delightful, his demeanor and posture changed.

As time went by, Sean was able to visit his parents and maintain his composure. There was a very symbolic moment between him and his mother. She was cleaning out closets and brought him a box of his things from when he was involved in the church. She asked if he wanted any of them, implying that she was okay if he didn't. He sorted through the box and took what he wanted and left the rest behind. It's a great metaphor: Take what we need, and leave the rest behind!

THE COMPLEX MAZE

There are no quick solutions regarding how to reconcile the challenges that come with religion. Gay men will have various individual needs, and subsequently, the solutions have to be tailored specifically for them. Imagine that there is a maze with many ways to enter and exit. Some turns lead to dead ends, and other routes wind their way in confusing directions but somehow end up getting to an opening. Each person needs to find his way, to chart his own course and, with some uncertainty, work his way out to the other side. Accepting the pain and struggles while maintaining a sense of control is the way out of the maze, no matter which opening one chooses.

Treatment goals may not be easy to attain, but you can help guide your client through his own maze. His self-image may have been chipped away at or completely decimated by a strict religious upbringing. At the same time, he may yearn for a way to practice the faith that has stayed with him despite its various messages, both negative and positive. This is an important balance to help him maintain, allowing him to release negative internalizations and at the same time reclaim the beliefs that continue to have meaning. Thus, helping your client make choices that promote self-esteem and comfort are necessary goals. Increasing your client's involvement with community, family, and institutions while helping him walk away from the groups that promote alienation and shame is the path to freedom. Experiential work that is creative and utilizes your client's way of seeing things will be the most effective of interventions as he begins to discover and then embrace this new path.

EXPERIENTIAL WORK

The premise of the following script, A Strong Foundation, is that every building needs a solid foundation. A solid foundation is durable and stable, allowing what is built on it to depend on its support no matter what is happening around it. An unsafe or unstable foundation is unreliable, and this metaphor describes the dilemma in which many gay men find themselves: The foundation is unstable with respect to the life they want to build, appearing to only offer support if certain conditions are met, conditions that require them to turn their backs on themselves. Thus, a new foundation must be laid, one that encompasses more elements than those that were acknowledged in the past.

A STRONG FOUNDATION

Start with a basic induction. Once the client is sufficiently relaxed, invite him to think about the foundation of a building:

"Imagine facing or looking at a building. This building that you see is solid and strong. Notice what this building looks like. What it is made of? Stone? Wood? Brick? Cement? What color is the building? Notice what the doors and windows look like."

[Have him report what he sees, and work with his images.]

"Now, as you get closer to this building, you can see the place where the foundation meets the ground floor. Right. This building is in good shape because it has a strong, solid foundation. The foundation is important because it keeps this building sturdy and level. It actually minimizes any damage from the outside and provides structural support to the rest of the building, the part that remains untouched. That is right.

This building can withstand storms, rain, winds, frost, and snow. You can truly appreciate just how many storms this building has weathered. Having a strong foundation means that the entire building, the whole of the building, is strong. That is right.

Just like the building, your own solid foundation supports a strength within yourself. You can really appreciate that when both of your feet are on the ground and the ground is level beneath your feet, you are unwavering and strong due to your own solid foundation. Appreciate what you notice inside your body in this moment. Excellent."

CREATE YOUR OWN SCRIPT

Remember that the power of creative mindfulness is in the utilization of what is at hand and your own spontaneity. We need to be receptive to what clients bring and be open to utilizing it in our experiential work and parts work. Using clients' metaphors and experiences helps direct them in ways that naturally resonate. Clients will appreciate the use of their imagery, language, and insights instead of you telling them how to feel. They will benefit by you guiding them to appreciate that they can use their own awareness to disentangle their beliefs from those of others so that uncertainty can be replaced with clarity. Emphasizing the validity of their knowing while using your own knowing collaboratively instills confidence and fosters growth.

_____

_____

_____

_____

_____

_____

_____

_____

_____

_____

_____

_____

_____

_____

_____

_____

_____

_____

_____

_____

_____

INTEGRATION OF PAST AND PRESENT

For many gay men, the dichotomy between their sexuality and their religion has created profound internal separation, a dissociation. As a therapist, you know that there are healthier, more comfortable ways of living. The ultimate answer is integration.

Integration means different things to different people. With regard to religion, it may mean that the client begins to broaden his sense of a loving god, allowing it to transcend the narrow interpretations and manipulations of human beings. For other clients, it may mean that they walk away from the religion of their youth, briefly mourning the specific loss but then being free to find new communities of faith that accept and celebrate them. For still others, inner peace may be found within a spiritual practice that is far from their original religion on one level but shares its attention to what is beyond the mundane tasks of the ego. Finally, some gay men may choose to walk away from any ostensibly spiritual path but still may search for a way to contemplate, to reflect, to "pray." No matter what the chosen path, mindfulness is key to integration—of the past and the present, the no longer relevant and the emerging, and the best of what was with the expanding container for what is.

HELPING YOUR CLIENT INTEGRATE THE PAST AND THE PRESENT

- **Delineate a stance:** Explore with your client his current beliefs and whether he wants to establish or maintain a religious or spiritual practice. He may have avoided this topic entirely up until now. Guide him to internally amplify his own stance to increase certainty.

- **Decrease fragmentation:** Help your client clarify that any pain he experienced from his religious upbringing is in the past and may be left there. You can help him finally separate from his past and begin to appreciate in the present how far he has come.

- **Make room for all the parts:** Demonstrate to your client how to make space for all of his parts. He is more likely to be able to own more resourceful states like openness and confidence if he can incorporate the more vulnerable ones safely.

- **Accept grief:** Prepare your client for some grief and distress; there is always a sense of loss when one moves on. The question is not if, but when. Reassure him that this is normal and shouldn't undermine the progress he has made.

- **Strengthen the core:** Support the client's understanding that core strength comes from being able to know and delineate what is best for him. Instead of living by the rules of others, he can live in accord with his whole self, taking self-ownership and allowing the core self to emerge.

- **Establish internal cohesion:** Help your client to feel good about the ways he has healed himself. This is the lasting resolution, integration. He can be who he wants to be, integrating new, strong, healthy ways to live as a happy gay man with or without religion or spirituality.

The following worksheet can help the client discern what from his past may continue to affect his current circumstances and desires.

WHAT IS STILL PRESENT
FROM THE PAST?

DIRECTIONS: Circle the best answer and then sit with each answer to see if there is more to say.

1. Did you grow up hearing that God would punish you or others for being gay?

   Yes   No   I don't know

2. Do you harbor that worry now?

   Yes   No   I don't know

3. Are you attracted to a spiritual practice or community?

   Yes   No   I don't know

4. Do you find the thought of a god or universal force consoling?

   Yes   No   I don't know

5. Is there part of you that still feels shame when you remember the church/temple/mosque?

   Yes   No   I don't know

6. Is there a part of you that is angry that you care about religion/spirituality?

   Yes   No   I don't know

7. Is there a part of you that has turned away from all spirituality?

   Yes   No   I don't know

8. Can you still feel the young boy in you?

   Yes   No   I don't know

9. Do you have compassion for him?

   Yes   No   I don't know

10. What is the part of you that has room for all of your parts called?

   _____

THE ROLE OF PARTS WORK

With parts work, eliciting contrasting parts—fears and certainties, strengths and vulnerabilities, etc.—is very effective. You want to remind the client that he has within him healthy parts that know how to provide good self-care. You can also remind your client that he has a part of him that is able to observe all parts. Most gay men pay more attention to their weakness and vulnerabilities, forgetting to notice strength. Being able to observe all parts allows access to both pain and strength and lets the client know that he can be on the lookout for the strong parts rather than focusing exclusively on what he sees as deficits. With regard to religion, you can help him enlist the parts of himself that can decide or that already know what he needs now in the present.

You can ask the client to identify and label parts of himself regarding his struggles. Better yet, you can use words that he uses to describe his parts and weave them into a script. This kind of customization will make the script more powerful, as it is more personal.

The following script introduces the concept of parts work as it will be used with the topic of religion, after which the client is invited to identify internal parts that are older and wiser and other parts that are younger and less mature. The goal is to achieve internal reconciliation regarding conflicts so that the client is freer to create a more realistic, more present-centered way to incorporate religious, spiritual, or other practices into his life. The integration of various parts allows for the steady foundation we talked about earlier so that what he builds now can be stable and expanded as needed.

You may decide to invite the client's various parts to speak with each other. Allowing all of the voices to interact may be just what he needs to assert a more present-oriented perspective. This approach helps to collapse time for a moment so that what is now—a time to recognize all that the client has gathered and built—can be acknowledged. The client will have the opportunity to experience that the present part, the adult part, has the capacity to feel compassion for, without being driven by, the past or the younger part. In neglecting the younger part, the client continues to suffer from the suppression of his pain and continues to let the past secretly inform his decisions. Integration means that no part is silenced:

- What does the child part have to say to the adult part about how the client has suffered or felt alone?
- Instead of the adult part ignoring or dismissing the child part (which is common), ask the adult part to really to listen attentively to what the child part needs.
- Encourage the child part to expose hurts and vulnerabilities to the adult part.
- Ask the adult part whether he is in a position to offer protection to the child part.
- Ask the adult part to speak to the child part, offering protection and recognition, so that the child part can listen and feel supported, understood, and most importantly, protected, perhaps for the very first time.
- Have the child part observe how it feels to be noticed and cared for, and have the client describe how it feels.

This can be quite powerful. Frequently, clients experience a turning point in their treatment during such moments. Integration comes from no longer splintering off parts that seem less evolved or undesirable.

Finally, the use of a mindfulness script will allow integration—the client's essential new compass—to be felt in the moment and then be the seed from which fresh resources can grow. The goal of integration isn't necessarily to make the client replace or recommit to any particular religious or spiritual path but to allow him to rest in a stance of his own heart and achieve the internal sense of unity that provides true comfort, no matter what choices are made.

Start with the emphasis of comfort inside his body. The key is for him to achieve comfort inside and then work from the inside out. Religious doctrine so often causes damage to the internal navigational system, trapping the gay man in me-versus-them trauma. The emergence of his internal wisdom as the most accurate navigation tool makes it easier to distinguish what he needs now.

Keep in mind that the difference between "sacred" and "scared" is the position of one letter. This is what you are offering your client: a way to shift his position, moving out of the past and into the full dimension of the present, out of fear and into confidence, from the stress that comes with fragmentation to the ease that comes with integration.

= SCRIPT =

BEGINNING TO INTEGRATE

"You know that it is really okay to not feel 100 percent certain about what to decide or how to proceed. You can function well, even though a part of you doesn't believe this. You don't need to minimize or hide your vulnerabilities. Instead, you can have all parts of yourself be present. That is right. You can really appreciate that you already possess what you need, and this inner knowing provides you with the truth that you can manage your struggles resourcefully. That is right. Even though you may have worked hard to minimize the part of you that feels vulnerable, you can remember that each part inside of you that makes you nervous or anxious, such as the vulnerable or the child part, is accompanied by an older, wiser part. Perhaps you have minimized this stronger part more than you need to, and now your strength can come out. Together, all of these parts, all of your own parts together, know just what you need in order to feel better and stronger. A little strength goes a very long way."

THE PATH OF INTEGRATION

"As you take these few moments, you can really appreciate what it means to go from the inside out. Think about it. Really get what it means, 'from the inside out.' You start inside. You take this moment to really enjoy being in the present. Identify experiences that you notice right now, from the inside out: What you feel, what you are aware of, and what comes from deep within are what matter most right now, while everything else feels more distant.

As you experience these joyful and comfortable sensations in your body, you identify aspects of your own uniqueness. It doesn't even matter what others around you experience or want for you. The sensations of now are your very own. Yes, that is right.

At first it may sound kind of odd, 'inside out,' because, when you put clothes on inside out, it doesn't look right, or maybe it doesn't feel right. When you look at yourself in the mirror, you see seams and labels that aren't where they belong. Yet, when you wear clothes in the proper way, you simply wear them and it feels right on the inside while hopefully looking good on the outside. You take various pieces from your wardrobe and put them together nicely to make an outfit, an outfit that is coordinated and matching. Integration consists of coming together internally, just like an outfit. That is right.

If you grew up in an environment where religion was important, perhaps you were taught that you needed to believe a certain way or needed to think that the way of others was the right way—or perhaps the only way. You were taught to think from the outside in. You may have incorporated external beliefs as your own, even if they weren't the healthiest for you. Perhaps you have spent a little too much time following the guidelines of others. If so, choosing a right outfit, your outfit, may have seemed difficult. However, now, during this moment of freedom, you experience a new way, a way in which you allow yourself to identify what it is that you want, what it is that you need, and what it is that you believe in, just for you. Yes, just for you and only for you. Options are more clear.

Think about a person whom you really respect. You have admired them, or maybe you have wished that you could achieve a certain integrity like them. Surely, they have been able to possess an assuredness that has caught your attention. *Imagine their strength, and now allow yourself to feel that same feeling inside of you, inside your body, as if it is your own. That is right. Feel it in this moment.*

As you do this, utilize this person as your role model, as your guide. Imagine this person standing by you, talking gently to you, guiding you to be your own strong, definitive person. That is right. This person leads you to a beautiful pathway, your path to integration. Enjoy what you see, the scenery, and allow yourself to move along. As you do, locate the space inside of yourself in which this person's strength, and now your strength, lives. Imagine that your body is solid and strong, strong and steady, and you are able to delineate what is best for you, what is right for you, feeling whole and complete.

Your path of integration consists of a coming together from an internal stance. Your body and your belief system are solid and strong, strong and steady, in a way that allows you to be able to delineate what is best for you and what is right for you. Excellent.

Just like when you try on clothing, you somehow know when it fits just right. Your body knows, and it feels really good. And even though faith is far more important than what you wear, your ability to discern what is best for you is now a skill that is innate—easy like choosing the right clothes for your particular body and occasion. Yes, that is right.

In this space of integration, you worry less about how others want you to be or what others think about you, and you focus more on where you bring yourself to and what you need and want for yourself. You are free, strong, and independent. This is your path.

Your spirituality comes from a sacred and special place inside. The place in your body where you feel strength. It may be in the middle of your belly, that soft space; or it may be in the center of your chest, your heart; or it may be near the top of your head, the wise place from which your thoughts radiate. Certainty comes from inside of now and works it way out!

You know how to grow beyond the beliefs of your family. Your pathway leads to your own private and sacred space. This is the place of internal beauty. What does it look like? Enjoy how you were able to get here, all by yourself. You establish your own rituals, which carry you along and which eventually you bring outside.

Here, you gather strength. This space is your den, your own cave, your own place for integration. That is right.

Although you may travel to various places outside in the world, where the landscapes may differ, cultures differ, and the rules differ, inside is your sanctuary—the place of knowing that allows integration.

When it comes to faith, what you believe is entirely up to you and only you. You choose what feels right for you.

You are who you want to be; you have found your way down this pathway, and here you are: a beautiful, bright place, a space all of our own—your sanctuary—healthy and strong, the place of integration. The wholeness inside connects you totally and fully—mind, body, and emotions. They are in unison, together, integrated. That is right."

7 | Toward a Generative Life

BEING GAY AND BEING HAPPY

Now you know more about gay men's lives and about how pivotal you can be in guiding your clients toward a fuller, richer life. You understand how and why mindfulness plays such an important role in wellness for gay men who learned early on to dissociate from the body to stay safe and to dissociate from their instincts, which have so often led to despair. You have committed to being sensitive and learning to appreciate the subtleties of your clients' struggles and successes. Since the goal is for each client to reclaim his strength, which may have been leeched from many directions, including history and repetitive internal reactions that are no longer needed, your creative guidance has been and will continue to be invaluable. These are the final pieces of your work: helping your client imagine and then welcome possibility; listening carefully in your sessions for the topics—to which he may allude in light and humorous ways—that still evoke feelings of diminishment and vulnerability; guiding him to stay alert, mindful of triggers, and committed to the practices of self-nourishment and gathering internal and external resources.

GOOD ACCOUNTING

The greatest rewards of doing psychotherapy come when we form intimate connections with our clients that help them soar. You can take pleasure in witnessing any and all movement toward greater well-being on your client's part; when he is strong, you can reflect that, and when he is not, you can stay with him. What we as therapists give is frequently appreciated in ways beyond what we can even comprehend. Hearing from clients, sometimes years later, thanking us for the difference we made in their lives is immensely gratifying.

MOVING FORWARD

For gay men, finding happiness can be complicated. There are so many threads connecting past and present, and while not all gay men have had the same upbringing, there are certain threads that are shared across most contexts:

- Growing up amidst disapproval of gay people and/or a lack of education about what it means to be gay
- Experiencing emotional or physical bullying in school, in the neighborhood, and sometimes in the family
- Living with the condemnation of the religious group to which the family belongs, and not being accepted by God

- The shame of being "different" and internalizing the images promoted by the bigotry of others

- Rejection or distance from the people who are supposed to provide love unconditionally

- The body being experienced as the enemy, leading the boy and then the man into unsafe and shameful territory

These threads are almost always connected to problems being experienced by gay clients in the present, even when they are masked by other issues, such as addiction or depression. Thus, the therapist uses this knowledge along with all the other knowledge he or she has gathered, including outside resources, strategies to build community, and activities that can foster healthier choices. Along with these tools, mindfulness practices may very well prove the linchpin to success. Experiential work can help clients untangle some of those finely knotted threads that confuse past and present as they consider the future.

Mindfulness holds that everyone has "core strength" that can be accessed under the right circumstances. Your practice can provide the circumstances. The core is the central, innermost part of the body: the place where balance and stability are first formed and the place from which they are transmitted elsewhere in the body. Movement starts at the core. Having a strong core means having a strong center. Some or all of the threads noted in the previous list have pushed and pulled at the gay male's core, sometimes wrapping around it and cutting him off from himself. The lack of acceptance or understanding from others is the earliest imprint on his self-esteem, and he carries this into the rest of his life. However, experiential work is a mighty approach, and through it, we can guide gay men back to reclaim their core strength. Once they have a sense of that possibility, they can build their muscles, no matter where they are in life, and move forward.

Happiness is accessible.

A Mindful Moment

Our clients have a pile of evidence that tells them that life is hopeless, that they are unwelcome, that connection puts us in jeopardy. These are old lessons—habits of thinking and feeling—that the practice of mindfulness can eventually overpower. You are helping your client create new evidence—that life is hopeful, he is welcome, and connection is affirming. You can remind your client about the progress he has made—and lay the groundwork for more.

Have him notice how easy it is to:

- Breathe deeply
- Enjoy the experience of practicing a moment of mindfulness in this moment
- Experience this moment as whole and blessed
- Smile
- Remember that these skills are his now

10 INSIGHTS ABOUT HAPPINESS

DIRECTIONS: Read each of the following opening statements and then answer the question that follows.

1. The comparing mind is always inaccurate. Comparing yourself to others creates feelings of inadequacy and disappointment. Instead, map your progress! How has your life changed for the better since you started on your own mindfulness journey?

    _____

    _____

2. Happiness comes from within; it emerges rather than being bestowed. Making good decisions regarding self-care protects that happiness. What can you do today that will feel like a good decision tomorrow?

    _____

    _____

3. Embracing who you are with confidence and care will radiate an energy that can be mirrored back. What would you like the world to know about you that you have kept hidden in the past?

    _____

    _____

4. A varied support network will be ready when you need it—one person or one group may not have all the answers. What connections can you imagine in the future, whether through an activity, an interest, or a shared concern?

    _____

    _____

5. Regular connection keeps the mind and heart open. Hosting dinners, book clubs, or other gatherings involves sharing yourself, your home, and your vitality with others. How might you create settings that are unique to you and welcoming to others?

_____

_____

_____

6. Being alone sometimes is good, allowing you to rebalance, rest, and turn inward. What's more, being comfortable with yourself is essential to true comfort in the world. What are some things you can do with time away from others?

_____

_____

_____

7. Giving back brings rewards. Altruistic activities improve mood and create a sense of purpose. What kind of volunteering might bring you contentment and allow you to feel appreciated for your special gifts?

_____

_____

_____

8. Creativity comes in all forms, whether making wardrobe or design choices or cooking, writing, or singing, and creativity is the juice of a vital life. What talents—perhaps long ignored—could you make time for now?

_____

_____

_____

9. Truly taking care of your body is part of taking care of your mind. A good diet, the right amount of sleep, and enough exercise support the beautiful, strong container that is you. What changes can you make starting now to show yourself love and compassion moving forward?

_____

_____

_____

10. A practice becomes a lifestyle. Continuing to use mindfulness strategies, including relaxation, body awareness, appreciation, breath work, and listening to scripts, will help you to feel centered and strong when you are not in the therapy office. What strategies do you like best thus far, and how will you use them?

_____

_____

_____

CHOSEN FAMILY

I support my clients in the notion of "chosen family": They can choose friendships that serve in the role of family. Often, these relationships are more relaxed or even closer than biological families because they are based on similar cultural norms and preferences. Often, there is a greater feeling of safety in the tribe of those who are like-minded.

Keith, who grew up in a loving family, experienced some trauma in high school when his family went through financial difficulties and needed to move. His parents' stress and heavier drinking led to Keith pulling away from his family for self-protection. Years later, he realizes why he has made his home a hub for warm friendly meals with his friends: He values the significance of his chosen family and treasures these experiences over anything else in his life. This is his first priority for happiness.

Most often, if you use the terminology of *chosen family* with your gay clients, they will automatically resonate with it, most likely because they have chosen family with whom they feel a special closeness. How refreshing and comforting when you see men who are close with other men—men with whom they can joke, argue, travel, and share aspects of life. For those gay men who have close ties with a healthy biological family, it is a double bonus to have chosen family as well. For others with more traumatic relationships with family, it is important to be able to rely on chosen family.

Creating a network of friends of all ages, genders, and races offers varying perspectives—about life, about family, about pleasure, about love. I encourage my gay male clients to enjoy their friendships with gay men but to expand beyond this bubble to enrich their lives even more.

THE INNER CIRCLE

Certain family members, as well as chosen family, have a place in therapy, too. I always enjoy how my clients spontaneously call on the support of their family or friends when in a trance state. All on their own, they find their way to their "inner circle" and enlist the people inside this circle to help empower their self-esteem and sense of feeling and being loved. Consider using the concept of the inner circle and presenting it to clients so they can explore the depths of its meaning. Who is in the inner circle? How large or intimate is it? What does it look like? Exploring the outer edges of the circle also provides an appreciation of friends and supports who may not be at the center but are nevertheless important. When you use the terms *chosen family* and *inner circle* regularly in your work with gay men, it reinforces the sense of the good fortune of having a supportive community alongside them.

This following script is a celebration of simply being who one is and having that appreciated by others. Given their years of internalizing messages of self-erasure and shame, my gay clients are especially moved by the images offered here. For those who crave the experience of being visible and affirmed, this script is especially potent.

Most gay men are familiar with a Gay Pride march, so referencing a parade likely already suggests internal pride.

Parade

"You are on an old-fashioned main street where there are crowds of people lined up along both sides of the street. Look around—notice what the buildings look like, appreciate the festive feeling of anticipation before the parade begins. Feel it in your body as well. Good.

You are in the parade, going down the street. Notice whether you are walking or you are in a car or other vehicle, whether you are inside or on top of it, or whether you are on a float. As you go down the street, bystanders are clapping, cheering, and waving at you. That is right. Just notice and appreciate how it feels to get this recognition.

Notice who is there. Are these folks who live in the town, or are they people who know you—friends, family, or other people who have been important to you? Are your closest friends and family there cheering you on? What messages do they have for you? Enjoy the sounds as they loudly shout out their praise. That is right.

Appreciate how it feels to be in the center of all this—really allow yourself to take it in. Sometimes you may feel self-conscious about receiving all this praise, but in this moment you enjoy the festivities, and it feels really good.

Notice what people are saying to you, and as you watch them cheering you on, you can take in the feelings of people believing in you, and you can proudly believe in yourself. Feel it inside. That is right."

AGING WELL

The topic of generativity wouldn't be complete without discussing healthy aging. It is a topic that evokes fear, especially for many gay men. There is a tremendous amount of pressure to not age! Unfortunately, men who are only in their late 30s often are already concerned about aging. Appreciating maturity and wisdom, which only comes from the accumulation of life experiences, is key.

Concerns regarding the normal aging process are inevitable for everyone. For gay men, many of whom lack the support of family, the concerns are especially pointed. Our role as therapists can be essential as our clients anticipate reaching later life. We have the vista from which to remind them of their accomplishments, to highlight the rich and colorful tapestry of life thus far, and to guide them in discovering new pockets of contentment and ease in these moments.

My clients appreciate what I do for them, and still, I am often the one who is learning. I particularly love my work with older gay men. I have the honor of hearing about their history— to hear their stories. Having respect for one's elders is not simply a platitude from childhood; it is the stance from which to be able to receive the wisdom of those who have gained the perspective that only time can offer.

Your willingness to serve as an advocate can be important. One thing you should be prepared to offer is information about services that are welcoming to gay clients. You may be the only person to whom your client has come out, particularly in the healthcare setting. The general instinct to hide, especially when it comes to medical care, can be mitigated by your advocacy. As clients age, there is even greater urgency for finding proper medical care.

A LIFESTYLE TRANSITION

The daunting question that looms for gay men who don't have kids is how they will be taken care of when they are older. This question usually comes up much earlier than is necessary, frequently arising for men in their 40s and 50s.

For older men, who are in the process of facing shifts in their independence, arrangements have to be made for daily assistance in various domains. This is a pivotal moment when a therapist's support and guidance can mean the difference between being prepared and being ambushed by sudden changes in health and ability. For men, the tendency to be stoic or minimize health concerns is common. Your objectivity will be received well and can help interrupt tendencies toward avoidance when it comes to important decisions.

It is hard to lose independence, and the more assistance that is needed, the more challenging the situation. Where a gay man decides to live as he ages has wide-ranging consequences; ideally, the move will keep him near friends or family. If this isn't possible, making sure there are gay neighbors or gay-affirming neighbors will help smooth the adjustment. In looking for assisted living facilities that are comfortable for gay men, important components include staff members who are welcoming and not homophobic, residents who are gay or have been exposed to gay men, liberal educational programs, and, of course, an attractive design and good food!

Don't forget that older gay male clients may need resources they won't ask for, so you can be the one who points them in the right direction. You will create a warm and open environment where information, resources, and suggestions for arranging legal matters, such as living wills and power of attorney, are displayed.

In the course of therapy, the rapport with your client that you have established will allow you to offer support and assistance in his making decisions involving end-of-life care, including funeral arrangements. You will be in a very special position to be able to encourage contentment at every stage. Older gay males' lives will be enhanced by appreciating and being involved in social, community, and creative activities that draw on their wisdom and experience to give back to others.

I recall one client who said, "I moved in to my assisted living facility and stepped right back into the closet." How disheartening to come to this stage of life and feel as though nothing has changed! However, my relationship with him allowed me to help him find his way back out of that closet and into better connection. He knew there was a way, but he needed someone to remind him.

MIRROR, MIRROR ON THE WALL: A TIME FOR REFLECTION

The stage of older adulthood is a time when individuals can look back on their lives and reflect on how they have lived, where they felt successful, and what they may have contributed to the greater good. This positive sense of accomplishment makes it easier to deal with the possibility of illness and the inevitability of death. Greater authenticity and deeper meaning replace the more superficial aspects of appearance and status. This is a goal for which we should strive with our clients at this life stage.

Gay men who are successful in this phase often reflect on the closeness they have had with their families, or they deepen their acceptance of not having reconciled with them. The embracing of other people in clients' lives can be remembered and celebrated to expand their feelings of contentment and peace. They may also review their career successes, the things of beauty they have collected, and their overall positive experiences. Many find that in the end, their "road less traveled" was a truly scenic route, and they can feel gratitude. Some clients will be able to attain this awareness easily, whereas others, especially those with a trauma history or mood disorder, will need extra help in finding ways to accept their painful pasts and create meaning in the present.

OLDER AND, YES, WISER

DIRECTIONS: Answer the following questions as though you are being interviewed by your younger self:

What is the sweetest memory you have of childhood?

_____

_____

What is your proudest accomplishment?

_____

_____

Did you take any unusual turns in life?

_____

_____

Who is the most interesting person you have known?

_____

_____

How have you made a difference to others?

_____

_____

Do you know that I am grateful to you, and do you know why?

_____

_____

What are the lessons you have taught me, so I can leave a legacy?

_____

_____

SIMPLIFY

The desire to simplify life in older age is common. Among other things, this can include a certain amount of clearing. Many therapy sessions may be devoted to the nostalgic review of the history of a client's treasures—where they are from, and what stories accompany them. Now what? Being able to give them to younger friends and family members who will appreciate them will be bittersweet. You will feel the depth hidden in this practical task immediately, and so will he, as the past connects to the present and the present hints at the future.

I recall so clearly during a visit with an aging client the poignancy and significance of emptying out his home. My seeing his beautiful house and appreciating his collections were very touching to him. He didn't have close family with whom to share the experience, and it was truly my pleasure to stand with him at this juncture.

Recently, I used hypnosis with a vibrant, healthy client in his early 70s. He was feeling depressed, and week after week, he was unable to shake it. His life was moving along fine, except that his house was on the market. He was slowly giving away his prized possessions to family members and friends, and he was donating pieces to various organizations. This all felt great, but he simultaneously sensed that he hadn't gotten to a piece of his core pain.

When we explored this in trance, a deeper layer of his unconscious truth quickly emerged. He shared, "I've gotten old. I have had a really good life, but there is something about me, about my life, that I need to share. I fear that if I don't share what I have learned, my life will mean nothing. My worth in life is to leave a legacy and pass on beautiful things that I have learned about life."

Recognizing this missing piece was a relief for him. He had time to work on this, and as a result of this session, his goal was to find a way to share his knowledge with younger people in his life.

PREPARE WHILE YOU CAN

Even if it seems premature, now is exactly the time to make arrangements for the future—and death is in the future for all of us. For therapists, it's important to note that gay men who do not have children tend to have a distorted sense that they will not have a legacy of any value. This is part of the historical piece of growing up feeling like outsiders, with nothing of weight to contribute.

Gay men who have not been financially successful may also feel inadequate in not being able to leave behind much of a material legacy. It's important to remind your clients that they may leave behind rich legacies of which they may not even be aware. You are the perfect person to help them understand the ways in which they have touched others in personal ways, through work, or via their various kindnesses. These legacies, the ones that are not measured in dollars and cents, are the ones that will be recalled over time, and clients can feel deeply satisfied knowing that their lives have been worthwhile and will have reverberations into the future. Not everything is measured by material success. You can help your clients see—and feel—this.

On a practical note, many people don't realize that if they do not create a will, it is the next of kin who will make decisions about their estate. If a client is estranged from his family, the idea that the family will have greater decision-making power than his friends or even his partner can be devastating. The therapist is in the position to encourage the client to prepare for making decisions about his affairs following his death. Emotional readiness and practical preparation go hand in hand. As clients age, we can help them think about decisions that will ease anxiety about the future.

PREPARING FOR THIS PART OF THE JOURNEY

The issues discussed here are among the many that will come up with older clients. Although this book deals specifically with gay clients, several of the questions to ask are appropriate for all of us:

- How can I simplify my world so as not leave a burden for others?
- Since I don't have kids, who will take care of me when I am sick?
- Should I tell my various healthcare providers that I am gay?
- Where will I live when I can't live independently?
- Are there assisted living options that are gay friendly?
- Who will make decisions on my behalf when that becomes necessary?
- How should I think about my will with regard to family and chosen family?
- What kind of arrangements should I make, given that I have left behind my family's religious traditions?
- Should I be buried in a family plot?
- What should I instruct people to do with my remains if I choose not to be buried?

These are topics that are often not discussed. Avoidance is a popular choice. As therapists, we want to help to raise awareness around these and other questions as clients age. Preparation is key.

> ### WE ALSO CAN STEP IN AS WITNESSES, HELPING CLIENTS TO ORGANIZE THEIR PREFERENCES AND MAKE THEM KNOWN:
>
> - Encourage your client to think about what he wants to happen to his possessions. Record this somewhere.
> - Work with your client to figure out what kind of service he would like to have to mark his passing.
> - Invite him to write his own eulogy or to review the accomplishments and/or attributes he wants to be incorporated into the eulogy. Think about the best person to deliver it.
> - Talk about how he wants his remains dealt with and record these decisions, including what he wants done with his ashes if he chooses cremation.
> - Most importantly, have him establish a will in which everything is spelled out legally. Creating a will ensures that all that he has gathered in life is gifted in the way he wishes on his passing.

USING MINDFULNESS WITH AGING CLIENTS

Seniors seem to enjoy mindfulness work even more than their younger counterparts. The depth of absorption in older clients is amazing, as if they earned the ability and privilege to go deeply into joy. Pain goes away, distractions disappear, and it is a welcomed relief for clients to return to their center, to their core.

The totality and culmination of life's wonderful experiences are automatically accessible and appreciated in the moment. I can see it on the faces and in the postures of older clients. Often, they comment that this is the first time they have ever been able to enjoy the benefits of going inside to feel serenity. Having the ability to appreciate this now allows them to open the door to history—and to unwrapping the present, including exercise, cultural activities, creativity, contribution, interest in other people, and anything else that may enrich the now.

As painful as it is to face, as our clients age and feel the closeness of their mortality, our role is to help them during this time, even as it brings up our own questions about mortality. As I worked with a client, Jeffrey, I took on a variety of roles: therapist, friend, family member, and doctor. The only time that Jeffrey really felt content was when he practiced mindfulness in my presence. A gentle smile would come over his face, and the usual obsessive worry would soften as he entered the internal relaxing world. His skills in practicing mindfulness seemed as instrumental as my caring.

Looking back, much of my work with him was related to his acceptance of aging. The loss of his long-term partner, preparing for what was ahead, letting go of possessions, and his diminishing looks were painful topics for him. The use of imagery, the incorporation of scenes involving nature, and the inclusion of relaxation were some of the gems that enriched our interactions and empowered him to be in accord with this life stage.

HAND-IN-HAND: OPTIMISM AND GENERATIVITY

Living well means having the ability to experience optimism, even in moments of pain. Our goals in helping clients include gently redirecting them from pain and toward possibility. The most endearing moments in psychotherapy occur when we watch our clients make this shift. Being able to cope with struggles while finding hope is a profound experience. Sometimes, this may involve finding an internal anchor; other times, the ability may emerge as a result of our gently reminding clients of their good fortune in being loved by a handful of wonderful people—the people of their inner circle. Using your own creativity and encouraging your clients to do the same are tools for helping clients experience optimism.

The following script may be adapted for specific clients and circumstances and to your own communication style. The experience of deep comfort can bolster feelings of serenity and hopefulness. Living well means different things to different people, but certainly it means being in accord with reality as it is. For gay men, this may require enlisting resources beyond the status quo.

Inner Circle

Start with a basic induction, and then continue as follows.

"Imagine a beautiful large circle, perhaps in the sand or in an open field. You might even imagine one that has been assembled with various stones. You can choose a place that is just right for you, a wonderful place outdoors or indoors.

Look all around you and appreciate the beauty of these surroundings. Take in the sounds and smells or simply notice the textures and the edges of this circle. Appreciate that inside of this circle is a space that is contained and sacred; your safety net.

Now, just notice that there is an opening to this circle. Perhaps it is a gate or simply a small opening where people can intentionally enter, with your permission. And you know that you are the gatekeeper of this inner circle. You allow those who deserve to be with you to enter through this opening, and you do well in maintaining the protection that you need between the outside and the inside world. That is right."

[If you need details about the client's vision of the circle, you can ask him to describe this place.]

"This is the place where your closest friends, chosen family, or biological family are next to you during very important moments in your lifetime—perhaps during happy moments, but also during times of pain and vulnerability. These may have been moments in the past or moments that will take place in your future. This is the place where support is generous, just for you. That is right.

Just notice who is with you—how each person looks, the expression on his or her face, and how they are situated inside of your inner circle. Excellent. You can also notice their body language as they tend to your needs inside of this special place. Who is standing around you? What are the ways in which they surround you? Appreciate how wonderful it feels to have them around you in this circle. As they surround you, you can experience the powerful strength of each and every one of these relationships.

Enjoy what you are experiencing in this moment. Appreciate where you feel these special feelings inside of your body. Excellent. This place, inside your body, is the place you will remember—being in your own inner circle, encircled by these special people who will give you just what you need—in each and every moment when you need it. You feel a wholeness now in your core. You and these people are together in the present; they are with you in the future, too. All is well. That is right."

As you work with your client, a shift in his awareness will energize him and excite you as well. During proud moments like these, we are reminded of our own gifts; our own generativity is received and appreciated. We are often reminded why we love working in this profession and how gratifying it can be. The richness in life comes through mutuality and caring. There is no need to stop when the going gets good: Continue using powerful scripts with your clients to amplify contentment. Maintain steady movement toward wellness.

This next script is designed to honor progress, to look back at accomplishments, while anticipating further growth to come. The title of the script comes from my former supervisee, Irwin Michelfelder, who ended each supervision session with a twinkle in his eye and a big smile on his face as he declared, "Onwards and upwards."

Onwards and Upwards

Following a general relaxation, read the following:

"In this moment, you can appreciate how good it feels to be relaxed and fully present. You are feeling fully satisfied; enjoy this feeling of being fulfilled.

And as you are ready, imagine that you are about to go on a beautiful hike into the hills that lie before you. Some are lower, and others are taller. You have packed a bag with snacks and water; you are well prepared for your time ahead, so you move along.

Begin heading up into the hills at a pace that feels perfect for you. That's right. And as you head up into these hills, you enjoy the ways in which the path winds around and around, along the perimeter of the hills, moving up gradually and slowly, onwards and upwards. Along the way, there are small clearings with lookouts, and you stop whenever you choose to, appreciating how far along you have come. As you look behind, you realize how far up you truly are."

[Ask the client to describe and elaborate on what he sees.]

"You continue moving forward. You see the space where the tops of the trees meet the sky, and you feel excitement about being as high up as you are. You have worked hard to get to this point.

Soon, you reach a large clearing. This is a place with beautiful views and a bench that entices you to sit, rest, and reflect. As you take a seat, you feel content with the progress you have made, and you enjoy the beauty that surrounds you. The views of where you have come from are impressive; so are the gentle sounds coming from below. Take it all in. That is right.

You appreciate where you have come from and how beautiful the environment is as you look ahead to the landscape in front of you. See yourself in this place, your future.

Your wishes and your dreams are accessible to you now, and you can really appreciate that what you want is within your reach. That is right. There may have been moments in your past when a part of you knew that what you wished for wouldn't become yours, but things are different now. You can reach your destination, which is just a little bit closer ahead. You trust and allow your hopes and dreams to be accessible now.

You can be realistic in this place, and it feels really good to know that what you want, you deserve and what you deserve can easily be yours. Excellent."

DEAR THERAPIST

I share this workbook to remind you (and all of us) about the importance of continuing to educate ourselves. Although society has become a more welcoming place for gay men, there is still a lot of work to be done. Our social and political parameters have broadened only relatively recently, and history looms large. Of course, there is still tremendous bias and ignorance. As you come to the close of this workbook, view its message as an invitation: to really get know the dimensions of what it means to be a gay man in therapy so you can be the most effective therapist for him. Understanding the deep and complicated background of all gay men— including the myriad consequences of growing up a minority even in one's own family; the subtle defenses developed to navigate rejecting family members, schoolmates, authority figures, and others; and the ways in which self-identity takes shape when there is no mirror—is integral to effective therapy.

A therapeutic repertoire that includes a layer of mindful connection will enhance and accelerate the healing process. Why? Because gay men—and arguably all clients—benefit from therapy that offers not just insight but also a way to embody insight so that it may be felt, appreciated, and then applied outside of the therapy room. Feelings of isolation, frustration, low self-esteem, and whatever else may be in operation can be met and reorganized experientially as clients allow new feelings—of connection, serenity, confidence—to take root.

Pathology is easy to understand and experience. Clients who had previous therapy most likely got this concept down. Now, you provide something new: hope, optimism, and a connection within the body. Out of your connection with your gay client and your sensitivity to his background will emerge creatively attuned scripts and activities. I have simply provided examples to get you started.

In bringing experiential work to your gay male clients, you will be offering a gift that may have no precedent in their lives: an open invitation to be full, whole, and free. Remember that the separation between body and mind is pronounced when the body has always been seen as an untrustworthy and even dangerous place. Experiential approaches invite clients to return to the body as it now begins to provide feelings of ease and acceptance, the mindfulness connection. Use your creativity to allow this to flourish.

Creative collaboration with your clients is an endlessly stimulating process—for them and for you. In holding up a mirror that reflects back clearly, with the old dust and distortion wiped away, you collude with a client's burgeoning sense of new possibility, his new home.

Home can be the place that you go to at the end of a very satisfying day, a wonderful place of restoration and renewal, a place for quiet. It may be the place you guide your client toward, a place of satisfaction and comfort that comes with decent hard work.

You may realize that the many tools that you now possess for helping clients move from pain to satisfaction are relevant to you as well.

Use this final script with your clients, and use it for yourself. Returning home can be one of the most satisfying experiences, having done the work and now deserving this rest and the feeling of joy. You may appreciate the metaphors in this script. **Welcome home**.

HOME

"You have been traveling, and your trip is nearing completion. This is a journey that no longer feels new; in fact, this is a journey that you can even take with your eyes closed. As you enjoy the experience of having your eyes closed, you feel the opposite of closed . . . wide open.

Imagine that as your destination is closer within reach, the familiar feelings and sounds entice you. A feeling of familiarity and peace comes over you—like driving down the road to your home with the satisfaction of knowing you have arrived at your destination. The feelings of relief are yours to enjoy now. Imagine the countless times you have come home—how as you get closer, that peaceful easy feeling is felt and now is embedded inside your body. That is right.

Before you go inside, appreciate the tranquil feeling that you have and imagine looking up at the sky on a very clear night. The stars are sparkling in the sky, reminding you of the vast beauty that surrounds you.

Home. It is such a magical concept—like being a child who is happy to be embraced by his welcoming family or a pet who excitedly reunites with its master, regardless of how long or how short the separation has been. Home is being in the space that feels familiar and just right. Three simple words—You Are Home. Excellent.

Home contains so many meanings. Yes, not only is your home the structure where you reside, but it also is the space that includes many complex and intimate levels. Home offers you shelter, protection, and warmth. It is a place to be safe and to grow. It is a place and a feeling.

As you open the door, the calm familiarity of comfort and peace awaits you. You come in, kick off your shoes, adjust the lighting, and enjoy that perfect feeling . . . there is no place like home. That is right.